Wordweaving

About the author

Trevor Silvester is a practising hypnotherapist in Berkshire, England. He is the editor of the *Hypnotherapy Journal*, and Training Director of The Quest Institute, a company that runs courses in Cognitive Hypnotherapy and Neuro Linguistic Programming. He is a Fellow of both the National Council for Hypnotherapy and the Hypnotherapy Society, and a director of the United Kingdom Confederation of Hypnotherapy Organisations.

To my wife Rebecca, for everything
xx

To my sons Mark and Stuart, 'Live, love, laugh,
and leave a legacy.'

Wordweaving

The Science of Suggestion

A Comprehensive Guide to Creating Hypnotic Language

Foreword by Dr Shaun Brookhouse

THE QUEST INSTITUTE

Text copyright © Trevor Silvester 2003
First published by The Quest Institute 2003
Berkley House, Bower Way
Cippenham, Slough
Berks, England, SL1 5HW

The author can be contacted on email
Trevor@questinstitute.co.uk
www.questinstitute.co.uk

British Library Cataloguing in Publication Data
A catalogue record for this book is available from the British Library

ISBN 0-9543664-0-9

Typeset by Amolibros, Watchet, Somerset
This book production has been managed by Amolibros
Printed and bound by T J International Ltd, Padstow, Cornwall, UK

Contents

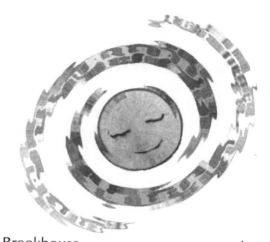

Foreword

It is a great honour and privilege for me to be writing the foreword to this important new volume by Trevor Silvester. I am often asked, 'What makes hypnosis more than just talking to someone with their eyes closed?' I have spent much of my professional life looking to answer that seemingly simple question.

Opinions are divided as to what makes hypnosis work or not, yet one thing that remains a constant is that great hypnotists and hypnotherapists have a wonderful command of language. It is my assertion that it is this mastery of language that makes hypnosis effective as a therapeutic modality.

With so many new texts on the subject of hypnotherapy it is important, I believe, to put this work into the context of the continuum of hypnotic literature. Many of the original textbooks on the subject were written by British professionals. Starting in 1843, *Neurypnology* by James Braid was the first great book on hypnosis – in fact it was in this work that hypnosis is reputed to have got its name. Shortly thereafter, in 1846, James Esdaile wrote *Mesmerism in India*, which looked at medical possibilities of mesmerism (hypnosis) in the treatment of pain and for surgical procedures. In 1903, British Physician Milne Bramwell wrote the historical and theoretical work on hypnosis, *Hypnotism: Its History Practice and Theory*. In these early texts, hypnosis was looked at in a fairly procedural manner, without much, if any thought regarding how hypnotic language works.

In the early to mid-twentieth century, the literature on hypnosis was dominated by American practitioners. The most widely read of these, and arguably the most widely published, was Milton H Erickson, MD. At this point in the history of hypnosis the power of language as the key to its effect first started to be looked at in much greater detail. In his works *Time Distortion in Hypnosis* (1954) and *Practical Application of Medical and Dental Hypnosis* (1961) Erickson began to look at the nuances of language in hypnosis. This trend continued in the 1960s with the publication of Dave Elman's *Findings in Hypnosis* (1964) and in the classic British textbook *Medical and Dental Hypnosis and Its Clinical Applications* by Dr John Hartland (1966).

In 1975 the proper study of hypnotic language was researched by Richard Bandler and John Grinder in the text *Patterns of the Hypnotic Language Techniques of Milton H Erickson MD* (two volumes). These researchers codified the linguistic patterns of the late Dr Milton H Erickson. It was a great leap forward, but the problem with it was one needed a working knowledge of general semantics to understand it fully, which most hypnotherapists do not have. Its coding is taught on most neuro-linguistic programming (NLP) trainings worldwide as the Milton model, and from my experiences as a master trainer of NLP, very few of my contemporaries fully understand the nuances of hypnotic language patterns.

Trevor Silvester is a trainer who does. His pragmatic approach to hypnotic language is contained in this volume. It is, in my opinion, the first easily explained and complete coding of the phenomena of hypnotic language patterns. When I say easily explained, I would like to emphasise that does not mean simple. Silvester's theoretical approach to hypnotic language is comprehensive and extensive. Where he has succeeded where others have not is that he has been able to explain these concepts in a way that the reader will easily understand, and that also makes it easy to utilise it in one's clinical practice. To my mind there could be no better description of this approach than the one Silvester uses: wordweaving. In my opinion, Trevor Silvester's work is the most significant step in the understanding of hypnotic language since Bandler and Grinder's work in 1975.

Dear reader, please do not only read this book, absorb it. By doing this you will enhance your hypnotic abilities tenfold.

Shaun Brookhouse, MA(Ed), DCH, PhD, PGDHP, HPD, FNCH,
Chairman, National Council for Hypnotherapy,
June 2002, Manchester

Acknowledgements

The writing of this book is the culmination of a journey that began about ten years ago. Many people have helped shape the direction of that journey and contributed to the huge enjoyment I have experienced along the way. I cannot mention all of them, but I would like to pay tribute to some.

First mention must go to my grandfather, Fred Cook. Over many patient hours when I was a child he taught me chess and awoke my curiosity. He never let me forget what I could be.

> 'Though I know that you have gone I've never felt you leave.'

Adrian Greaves introduced me to hypnotherapy and was a great support while I took my first steps towards a new life.

To David Shephard and Tad James for giving me such an excellent grounding in NLP, and who really opened my eyes to what is possible. Without their teaching I could not have come so far so quickly.

Latterly to Gil Boyne. I have been privileged to have him as a mentor, and proud to call him a friend. He is a giant in the field of hypnotherapy who has taught me so much about so much.

My friends on the Committee of the National Council for

Hypnotherapy. They give their time freely and honourably to the development of our profession. I want to mention specifically Fiona Biddle for her support and assistance in vetting the manuscript and giving me excellent advice on its presentation. Also the chairman of the committee, my friend Shaun Brookhouse for contributing his kind foreword to the book, and his tireless efforts in promoting hypnotherapy.

Wordweaving™ would not have been possible without my students. I am privileged to have had the opportunity to teach them, and I want to particularly thank the pioneer classes of 9/01 and 11/01 at the Quest Institute for their patience, enthusiasm and support while I honed my ideas on them. I learnt a lot from you. This book began as a dream. Dream your dream and then make sure you act on it. It's the step most people miss.

Finally, to the student of mine who inspired the cover. Anthony Bennett is an inspiration to me. At the age of fifty-two he took early retirement to pursue the development of his talents. He is an accomplished pianist and an excellent artist. He became my student at the age of sixty-seven. I aspire to the curiosity that keeps him looking, his openness to ideas and his generosity of spirit. If he learnt as much from me about hypnotherapy as I learnt from him about living, I run a good course!

I hope you enjoy the book.

Trevor Silvester

Introduction

The purpose of suggestion

Words are magic – they always have been. Their ability to pass on knowledge has made our species pre-eminent on the planet. Words allow us to share our thoughts and build dreams. The skilled use of words has brought incredible power and bent the collective wills of entire nations to the whims of a single individual. It is said that before battle the Druids of opposing Celtic tribes would hurl spells and incantations at each other, and sometimes the loser would fall to the ground stone dead. As a hypnotherapist the potency of words sometimes amazes me. There have been days when a client's response to the words I have woven has changed his or her life, and often I've known it as I've heard myself say them. But there have also been days when my words have bounced off, and my client has continued in their limited version of reality. That is what this book is about – refining the power of words inherent in hypnotic suggestion to a point where more of our suggestions hit the mark, and fewer bounce off. This book presents a theory of suggestion that allows users to know specifically what their words are intended to achieve. It has evolved from my efforts to answer the most common question posed by my students:

> 'How do I know what to say? I'm scared I'll dry up in front of the client without a script.'

By following the ideas in this book not only will you never dry up, but every suggestion you make will be deliberately aimed at achieving a specific positive effect.

It is common to talk about hypnosis in magical terms, because the effects are often as close to magic as people ever experience outside of the cinema. In many respects I think the analogy is apt. The basis of magic is transformation, from one thing to another, from one place to another. So is the basis of therapy. Therapy is about transforming the nature of a client's experience into something that enhances the quality of his or her life. In that respect a hypnotic script acts as a spell – the medium by which the transformation is achieved. But I think this is where hypnotherapy has limited itself. The spell woven to send Sleeping Beauty to sleep was different from the one cast over Rumpelstiltskin. Similarly, the spell required to awaken them was specific to them and their situation. Yet this point is lost in much of mainstream hypnotherapy. A weight-loss script is applied in much the same way to each and every client seeking to lose weight. This is because hypnotherapists tend to have a book of scripts, and those who don't have usually memorised what they are going to say. The next smoker is given the same spell as the last. That is not the nature of magic.

As a hypnotherapist what you say to a client should have a point. I know that sounds obvious, but there are many therapists who make suggestions without a clear idea of what specific effect they are hoping to achieve. They may read a script from their book, or have written a script to fit a particular problem, but often the aim is general – to get a client to stop a behaviour, begin a new one or to 'ego-build'. By dealing in generalities the script is available for use on anyone with a similar problem, but will fit nobody perfectly. This may be a factor in the range of responses clients have to hypnosis. A 'smoking' script may stop one person from ever lighting another cigarette, but have absolutely no effect on another.

I believe that each suggestion you make to a client should be unique to the needs of that client, to act like a spell, woven

out of the material the client provides and aimed deliberately and specifically at achieving a particular response. For that reason this book begins with a bold statement, from which the science of suggestion will unfold, and from which the structure of hypnotic magic will be revealed – Wordweaving.™
The statement is this:

> Each person's reality is subjective, it is created by that person's own mind, and the purpose of any hypnotic suggestion is to change that person's perception of that reality.

If you do not keep this purpose in mind when developing a suggestion then any improvement in your client will be a result of accident or happy circumstance. Aimless suggestion is just being artlessly vague.

I am going to take you systematically through the way in which our minds create our individually unique view of the universe – our 'model of the world' – and particularly the way in which we create for ourselves a world in which we are limited. I will then show you how to build suggestions to remove those limitations, suggestions that act like a surgeon's scalpel, not like a sawn-off shotgun.

This book is written primarily for people working in the field of therapy, but might also prove useful to those who want to improve the quality of their communication skills. It is not intended as a 'read-only' text, but as a workbook that can be used to build your skill at weaving suggestions. Such skills need to be built incrementally, so wherever possible I am going to reduce ideas to processes, models that may not be true but that serve as a means to learn. Use them while they are useful. It is my hope that in a short space of time you will be 'wordweaving' without being consciously aware of how the elegant and effective suggestions that come out of your mouth are formed. Let us begin that journey with the three steps of the Wordweaving™ process.

The three steps of Wordweaving™

1 Identify what aspect of the client's experience your suggestion is aimed at changing.
2 Choose which mental processes, usually termed 'trance phenomena', should be used to achieve that shift in perception in your client.
3 Linguistically frame the suggestion to achieve that aim.

Each suggestion you make will contain elements from each of those steps, and this book is about helping you learn those elements, and how to combine them.

If the purpose of suggestion is to change perception then we need to begin by looking at how the mind gives meaning to experience in the first place. We need to know how we create our 'model of the world', in order to learn how to change it.

Part I

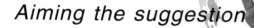

Aiming the suggestion

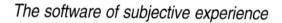

The software of subjective experience

We can never know reality. Evolution has provided us with a number of mechanisms through which we can be aware of four dimensions of the outside world. Those mechanisms are our senses. They are amazing tools that allow our brain to be aware of something like 2,000,000 pieces of information per second, yet they are still very limited in their ability to comprehend the whole richness of reality. As you sit reading this, there are colours around you that you cannot see, sounds you cannot hear, and smells you cannot smell. There's a better than even chance there may be universes around you we cannot comprehend.

The human race lives in a narrow band of reality that is quite different from the band of reality of a bee, or an ant or dog. As individuals we each construct a version of reality from within this narrow band of information, which will share many common components with that of other humans – we can all point at a spider and know it as a spider – but the model of reality we each create from this band of information will also be unique as to the meaning we give such objects. Some will want to keep the spider as a pet, others will want to squash it. We obviously do not all see the *same* spider.

As Epicetus stated, in 100 AD:

'Men are disturbed not by things, but by the views
which they take of them.'

So how do we gain our views? We get them from the way the
mind takes information from the senses and gives meaning to
it.

It is through our senses that we obtain the raw information
that our brain refines into our perceptions. The word 'refine'
here is key, because the brain acts as a reducing valve. While
unconsciously we can process something in the order of
2,000,000 bits of information from our senses per second,
research by George A Miller demonstrated that consciously
we can be aware of only seven plus-or-minus two bits of
information (this just means a number between five and nine)
at any one moment. It is easy to keep three different items in
our head at once; five is more difficult, and ten is a real stretch.
Miller wrote,

'There seems to be some limitations built into us
either by learning or by the design of our nervous
systems, a limit that keeps our channel capacities
in this general range.'[1]

This makes our awareness highly selective. You may not have
been aware of the tip of your left ear until I just mentioned it,
but you are now, aren't you? Before that moment the tip was
part of the 2,000,000 bits of information, but it was not admitted
to consciousness by your unconscious. Directing your attention
as I did made it part of the seven plus-or-minus two bits of
information at that moment. As you read that last sentence it
probably drifted out of your thoughts again. This happens to
all information moment by moment. It makes you wonder just
how much we don't notice around us. By the time something
percolates to the level of conscious awareness it has also been
refined and given meaning. For example, look at this picture.

The picture is two-dimensional and made up of shading and a number of lines and curves. Our unconscious will interpret this information and present it to our conscious mind. This is something it has learnt to do. Show this picture to someone who has never seen a picture before and he probably won't recognise the information in it. You may remember the film *In Plain Sight,* starring Val Kilmer, a fictionalised account of a true case where a man was given sight for the first time in his mid-thirties. When the bandages came off he was still blind even though his eyes were now perfect. It took a long time for him to 'make sense' of the patterns of light received by his retina and turn them into recognisable objects. Knowing the difference between an apple and a picture of an apple was just one of the many problems. In real life the man was unable to adapt and eventually committed suicide.

With this picture, some people will see a young woman, some will see an old hag . The point is that our consciousness, that part of us we identify as our 'self', is presented with the sense already made of the picture, and takes the interpretation to be its own doing. We are often not even aware that a choice has been made by another part of our mind. It is an uncomfortable fact to acknowledge that research suggests our unconscious is responsible for ninety per cent of our behaviour in any given day. It chooses the information we base our responses on, and often directs that response.

Gestalt theory talks of 'foreground' and 'background'. 'Foreground' is that information selected by the unconscious and which is brought to conscious awareness (the seven plus-or-minus two bits of information). 'Background' is all the other information available to the senses that is not chosen for our awareness, but which our unconscious can still respond to.[2] This is vital to our understanding of what we intend to achieve with our suggestions, because a client's problem is the result of one of two things:

1 The unconscious selecting those bits of information from the 'background', which equal 'the problem', and making them the foreground, e.g. people with a spider phobia walking into a room and seeing a spider on the carpet. All of the information that equals the spider fills their conscious awareness – it is now their foreground, to the exclusion of all other information – the background.

2 Responding to something that remains in the background, i.e. out of awareness of the client. An example of this is some anxiety attacks where the trigger is something of which the client remains unaware, something in her environment, or an over-sensitivity to a normal bodily experience, such as her heart beat, or a blush.

In both cases the client experiences a narrowing of attention that means the client is not aware of the vast amount of information that equals 'not the problem'. The purpose of suggestion is to re-educate the unconscious to do one of two things also.

The key purposes of suggestion

To have the unconscious not select or respond to information from the background that equals 'the problem';

or

To have the unconscious give that information a different meaning so that it equals 'not the problem'.

I want to introduce you to a model of the process the unconscious uses to dictate our responses to situations. Understanding this model takes us closer to knowing where to aim our suggestions.

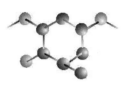

The Matrix Model

The Matrix Model is an attempt to map the mental steps the unconscious mind takes from the first moment it becomes aware of a need to consider or respond to information from our environment, to the completion of its response to that information. Those of you familiar with NLP will recognise it as a variation on the idea of *strategies*. We all have thousands of these processes that activate throughout our day. They are a part of the generalisations we make to free our attention. We have a strategy for mundane things like cleaning our teeth or tying our laces, just as we have a strategy for more complex behaviours, like solving a problem – or creating one. For the purposes of this book we will follow the model in the context of how people 'do' their problem, and we will use it as a means to give you background information on the way the mind is thought to work. That will give you a clearer insight into what your suggestions need to achieve. There are five steps within the Matrix Model.

STIMULUS

This is the external event, like spotting a spider, or mental activity, such as remembering or imagining something, which acts as a trigger for some other mental or physical activity or action.

MEMORY MATRIX

A matrix is a framework that holds information. In this model it describes the way the mind forms patterns of memories and uses them to create meaning, by comparing the stimulus to these patterns in order to find a match.

EMOTION

When a match is found it generates an emotional reaction.

RESPONSE

Depending on the emotion and its strength, a 'thought sequence' – and/or a behaviour based on the meaning generated by the matrix of memories matched to the present stimulus – results.

TERMINATION

The exit of that behaviour or thought sequence.

EVALUATION

An unconscious appraisal of the event sequence that confirms or denies its validity. ('That worked – and confirms what I think,' or 'That was different, what has changed?')

We will examine these five steps in more detail as the book progresses, and weave into the Matrix Model the three steps of suggestion. I will use an example to show how the model works:

THE CASE OF MRS TOOTHBRUSH

A forty-three-year-old female lawyer came to see me with an unusual phobia; she was terrified of toothbrushes. She had never been able to clean her teeth, or visit the dentist, without gagging or having a panic attack. Under hypnosis I regressed her to the origin of the problem. At eighteen months old she had swallowed deadly nightshade berries and been stomach pumped at the local hospital. Since that time she had developed a strong reaction against anything similar going into her mouth.

The sequence of her problem develops like this:

Stimulus: She walks into the bathroom to brush her teeth and sees the toothbrush.

MemoryMatrix: Her mind seeks a match of the toothbrush with previous experiences (as it will do with every other object in the room). The match is to the event at eighteen months. For reasons that will be explained later her unconscious has made a connection between the instrument used to pump her stomach, and the toothbrush.

Emotion: The *matrix match* generates a strong emotion – fear. This prompts our natural flight or fight response, which is interpreted as a panic attack.

Response: The actions that have developed over time in response to this stimulus is a gag response if it goes near her mouth, or a 'flight response' if at a dentist.

Termination: Her emotional reaction stops when the stimulus is no longer near her.

Evaluation: The evaluation in this case compares the thing that the unconscious is trying to avoid – the pain of being stomach-pumped – with the outcome of her response in the present. Each time she is able to avoid that historical pain the response is reinforced because, accord ing to the logic of the unconscious involved at the origin of the problem, it has been 'successful' – this an unconscious that at that moment continues to be eighteen months old. That will also be explained a little later (a blatant attempt to build curiosity and expectation!).

I am suggesting that every problem people bring to therapy, whether it is a phobia, a lack of confidence, or an eating disorder, involves this model *at the moment* of their *doing* their problem. Identifying each stage of the Matrix Model with each client's problem gives you points to aim your suggestions at.

Let's look at each point in more detail:

Stimulus – how we perceive a problem

We are aware of any external event only through our five senses, visual, auditory, kinaesthetic, olfactory, gustatory (VAKOG). The stimulus is the information received from the senses, which is given a meaning that requires a response to maintain our well-being. In the case of Mrs Toothbrush, the toothbrush is the stimulus, which in her model of the world constitutes a danger she has to respond to. The journey from external event (toothbrush) to internal meaning goes something like this:

Our unconscious begins to filter the 2,000,000 bits of information by selecting which sensory aspects surrounding us are either:

➤ The most powerful (i.e. if you fell in a sewer the thing you'd notice most would probably not be the colour of your surroundings!).

➤ Those most relevant to survival (in the view of your unconscious), *or*

➤ The aspects your preferred sensory system picks up. We each tend to pay more attention to one sense over others.

The stimulus is any information that is picked out via the senses for attention, or that has been generated by the mind itself, as with a memory or an imagined scenario.

With this first-stage filtering accomplished, the information arrives at a part of the brain called the thalamus, which is like a junction box. It sends the raw information to the areas of the brain that are responsible for processing it – such as visual information split into its components, colour, contrast, movement, etc.

Here is an interesting fact. When those areas of the brain send that information back to the thalamus, there is eighty per

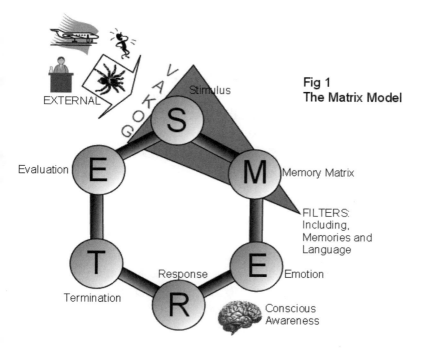

Fig 1
The Matrix Model

cent more information than when it was first relayed. Somehow the brain has added more information than it originally received. What this means, in essence, is that eighty per cent of what we perceive we 'make up'.[3]

By this I mean that we decide what we are perceiving, and perception depends on prior learning. When you look at a chair you recognise it as such only because you have seen countless others in the past. Show it to a child for the first time and she is as likely to try to eat it, smell it, or talk to it, as she is to sit in it. In the case of Mrs Toothbrush the eighty per cent of information she adds about the toothbrush to the raw information from her senses causes her to panic.

So what is this eighty per cent extra information and where does it come from? From the moment of our birth we have been building a model of the world, a model that defines how the world works in order for us to be able to navigate it safely. We use it as a map that contains borders and boundaries, places that are safe and places where there are dragons. By the time we are adults our model has been refined to a point where we are probably quite confident about how the world works. We don't step gingerly onto the floor in the morning in case it is no longer solid; we take it as a fact that there actually is a road beyond the immediate range of our headlamps because that was the case yesterday. We often mistake the map for reality. But, as Albert Korzybski famously pointed out in *Science and Sanity*,

'The map is not the territory it represents.'[4]

and most of us will have mistakes built in from when we were children. Bandler and Grinder in *The Structure of Magic* (vol 1) introduced an elegant set of tools to explain how we organise our experiences into this model of the world. They called them 'universal processes of human modelling'.[5] These processes are 'deletion', 'distortion', and 'generalisation'.

Universal modelling processes

Looking at the model in Figure 1 you will see that the Matrix Model uses the concept of filters, something it has in common with NLP. Our filters are responsible for what gets deleted, how things get distorted, and what generalisations we make. Over time these processes will form our belief systems about how the world works, and our place in it.

DELETION

You already know that the central nervous system receives about 2,000,000 bits of information every second. If every bit was evaluated equally it would probably take our whole lives to process the moment of our birth. That is where deletion comes in. Information passing through our filters is either judged to be unimportant or irrelevant and so is deleted before it reaches our conscious awareness. Were you aware of how your left ear was feeling until I mentioned it? Aldous Huxley writes in *The Doors of Perception*, experience

> 'has to be funnelled through the reducing valve of the brain and nervous system. What comes out the end is a measly trickle of the kind of consciousness which help us to stay alive on the surface of this particular planet.'[6]

This is echoed by the comparatively new science of evolutionary psychology, which seeks to explain our behaviour on the basis of its 'survival value'. If it doesn't have such a value the behaviour would not have survived.

All the cave people who stopped to process all 2,000,000 bits of the sabre-toothed tiger running at them died aeons ago. Taking a snapshot of reality helps to keep us safe. Ask someone you know to close her eyes and ask her to recall five bits of information from the environment around her, such as the colour of the wall, your shoes, etc. See how many she gets right. It is surprising how much of what is around us we disregard, while thinking we are aware of it.

In most people's model a toothbrush would probably be deleted from our awareness when we walk into a bathroom (i.e. not noticed), unless we were going to brush our teeth. Not so Mrs Toothbrush, when at some level her unconscious is making it into a sabre-toothed tiger, a 'distortion'.

DISTORTION

Have you ever failed to notice the change in appearance of someone close to you? A new hair style, the shaving off of a moustache? We will often see what we expect to see, and will twist what we are actually seeing into something that fits our model of the world. With the examples above, what happens is that the mind quickly recognises the pattern of light coming through the door as the familiar person (let's call her Fred) and will project onto the body of Fred what it expects to see. It might be some time before the difference bubbles into your awareness. In the study of perception a term used is the 'difference threshold'.[7] This is the minimum amount of stimulation necessary for the central nervous system to register a difference between two similar stimuli – such as how someone is looking, and how you remember her looking. If Fred comes home with her head shaved, then that will probably trigger the threshold and the difference will come into your awareness. If the change of style is not as stark, then the difference remains below threshold. It is why we only intermittently notice the ageing process in our partners and ourselves. The face you see in the mirror is the one you expect to see – unless you stop and look twice.

Another neural mechanism allied to this is 'recurrent inhibition',[8] which is the tendency to receive information from our senses primarily about changes in our environment rather than about constant or unchanging aspects of experience. Again this has a survival value. If you walk out of your cave and pay attention to the rock that has sat motionless outside for the last ten years, you may not notice the movement at the edge of your vision that is a tiger stalking its breakfast. It is why hypnotic suggestions should have the client focus on information that can be construed as change.

The relevance of this to suggestion

If recurrent inhibition and the difference threshold work to bring into our awareness only changes and differences beyond a certain degree, then it means that in normal circumstances these mechanisms will have the effect of maintaining the problem – it will 'be like it always has been'. As therapists we cannot always depend on the changes we achieve in the client to be instantly huge, so our suggestions should always be aimed at tuning the client's unconscious to notice *any* difference or change in his problem, and making that difference *mean* he is improving. Make a mental note of this point and we will return to how to do that specifically later on.

As with all three processes, distortion has its downsides. How many people have said after their partner has walked out on them, 'But we seemed so happy.' They saw what they wanted to see – what they had probably seen for the majority of their relationship. The drift to discontent was so gradual that it fell below the difference threshold, so that he/she never paused to give the relationship a closer inspection and just kept distorting the external event into what it was expected to be.

The phrase 'I couldn't believe my eyes' describes the moment when we are overwhelmed by something that falls outside the limits of our model of the world, which we just can't comprehend. When that happens people often freeze because they simply have no prepared behaviour. The experience is so dissimilar to any they have had before that the mind has no response to it. It is while it tries to come up with something that people experience that 'frozen' moment.

In the case of Mrs Toothbrush her unconscious is distorting an inanimate object into something that represents a danger to her. That is what most problems are, a distortion of available information into a particular negative form peculiar to the individual.

17

GENERALISATION

This process is part of the reason why we learn as quickly as we do. Our mind tends to learn by association. Anything we experience tends to be compared with previous experiences using three basic algorithms:

> $A = B$.   This is the same as that, known as a 'complex equivalence'.
> $A = $ not B.   This is different from that.
> $C > E$.   This is because of that, known as 'cause and effect'.

This ability means that we don't need to waste a lot of time treating each new experience as something completely novel, and trying out behaviours randomly to find out if they are appropriate. Instead we take bits and pieces of behaviour from previous experiences and synthesise them into a composite new behaviour. This new behaviour then provides the potential for comparison with some future experience.

The survival value is obvious. If a sabre-toothed tiger tried to eat you yesterday it is a useful generalisation to suppose it may do so again today. Generalisation is the basis of learning. Trying to learn something completely outside of your life experience is infinitely harder than learning something that is in any way similar to something you already know.

This search for patterns is hugely relevant to therapy and the structure of our suggestions, because it is very often bad generalisations made by the client's unconscious that are causing the problem (as I will explain when we get to the filter of memory). They often cause our model of the world to be inflexible. A memory matrix is held together by a generalisation, and we all have many thousands of such matrices, which, combined, form the master matrix that we call reality, but is really only our model of the world.

In the case of Mrs Toothbrush her eighteen-month-old

unconscious made the generalisation (A = B) that objects similar to the stomach-pump tool were dangerous to her. That generalisation became stronger each time her unconscious 'saved her' from a recurrence of the original trauma.

Psychologists did an experiment where they took 100 people at random and placed them in a room with a door. They offered them $10 if they could open the door. In every case the subject pushed the door, pulled it, and declared it locked. It wasn't. The door was designed with the hinges on the same side as the handle. Nobody had the flexibility to think 'Could this door work differently from every door I've ever used?'

As a therapist, or as just an interested observer of people, you come to notice how they get locked into patterns of behaviour and are unable to do anything else except repeat that pattern. It is strange but generally if people do something that has worked in the past, and this time it doesn't, the first thing they will do is the same thing again – but harder. I have had countless students coming to me who have said 'I was studying three hours a night, but only averaging sixty per cent in my exams, so I reckoned that if I studied for five hours a night I would get at least seventy-five per cent. But I didn't.' No wonder. They had a study method that wasn't working, so they just spent more time doing something that wasn't a success. If you are sailing in the wrong direction, sailing faster is not going to help! If something isn't working do something different, and keep doing things differently until you get the result you want (in NLP there is a saying I have tattooed on the inside of my eyelids:

There is no failure, only feedback.

Follow that principle with all your heart and it will transform your life).

To sum up. These three universal modelling processes are used on all information passing through your filters. They are how your filters filter.

The matrix and memory – how we know a problem is a problem.

If you cast your mind back, earlier the question was asked, 'Where does the additional eighty per cent of information come from in response to the work of the thalamus?' The answer is that it is largely perceptual information based on memory.

Can I begin by saying that the complexity of the brain is beyond our present ability to unravel. We do not know precisely how the brain works, or precisely how memory is encoded. What I am going to present is a model developed from the latest research.

We all have millions of memories. Some of us feel that we have a good memory, and have a great recollection of our youth, while others can hardly recall anything. Our preferred sensory system may have something to do with this. NLP suggests that our memories are encoded and stored in the brain according to their submodality qualities. Each of the VAKOG senses is a modality, so submodalities are the components of each modality, for example for the visual system the submodalities of a picture will include whether it is in black and white or colour, moving or still, three- or two-dimensional, etc. For the auditory system, volume, location and tone are examples of the submodalities that make up a sound.

A specific memory is not localised in a particular part of the brain, unlike a filing cabinet. It is actually spread around the brain in a number of different places. Imagine you are a speck at the centre of your brain system. Look up at the billions of brain cells and imagine them as stars in the sky. Look more closely and you will notice some conform to patterns, or constellations.

These constellations are individual memories, and each star is a submodality of that memory. Different memories will have a different balance of submodalities, which will affect the recall in each individual.

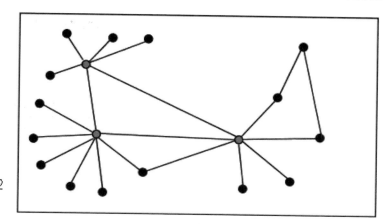

Fig 2

A 'visual' person will try to recall something by first accessing the visual qualities of the memory. This will provide the 'trigger' for remembering the whole memory. If the visual qualities of the memory are not strong the trigger will be weaker and so accessing the memory for them will be more difficult, or it may be 'forgotten'.

The clearest memories that people have will be ones with strong encoding in all the submodalities – sounds, pictures and feelings. It may be that some people whose strongest sensory system is kinaesthetic (feeling) have poor recall because their trigger will need to be a feeling, and only a few of our past experiences are likely to have a strong feeling associated with them.

From your view in the centre of the brain some of the constellations will be bright, others will be fainter. Viewed over time recent memories might be bright, and gradually fade. Others that are accessed regularly remain clearly visible (which is why revision works).

If you could look more closely you would see that the pattern is actually more intricate. Constellations connect to others, sometimes in a simple form, more often in complex, intricate webs. These are the memory strings, or matrices, we accumulate during our life as a result of the filter algorithms mentioned earlier $(A = B, C > E)$. They are connected by the meaning we give them. We experience these meaning patterns as 'beliefs'.

Imagine all of these matrices connected in a huge, interactive web. The sum total of this web is 'our galaxy' – our 'model of the world'. The number of connections between them is too staggering for us to comprehend, the crowning accomplishment of evolution. Throughout our lives these connections can continue to grow, which is the probable basis of wisdom. We might become slower at learning new things, but older people can often discern the 'big picture' better than the young. Life experience is the multiplicity of our neural connections.

So a matrix is a collection of memories linked together around a certain subject. The great NLP Trainer Tad James describes them as a 'string of pearls'. If you recall the story of Mrs Toothbrush you can see this in action. There is a first event that is given a particular meaning. Any future event that fulfils the algorithms $A = B$ (this is the same as that), or $C > E$ (this is because of that) is linked to the original and begins the pattern I refer to in this book as a matrix.

This matrix will have an emotional meaning, whether positive or negative, and often a pattern of behaviour, either to reduce the negativity (as in the gag reflex with Mrs Toothbrush), or maintain or increase the positivity – somebody who has a strong positive response to a childhood stage performance is likely to be motivated to jump at any opportunity to 'perform' in public in the future. It explains many of the terrible karaoke singers who seem oblivious to how bad they actually are – they are still hearing the childhood applause in their ears.

These behaviours can be controlled by the conscious mind, as long as the emotional response contained within the matrix does not exceed a certain threshold. If it does exceed that threshold the behaviour is taken over by the unconscious – the emotional brain – however inappropriate that behaviour may actually be in the present circumstances, and totally outside the person's conscious ability to control it (as in Mrs

Toothbrush's). This threshold will be exceeded if the matrix contains a 'significant emotional event' (SEE).

SIGNIFICANT EMOTIONAL EVENTS

There are four factors involved in whether an experience becomes an SEE, either the first 'priming', sensitising event, or one that gets attached to the chain later:[9]

1 The intensity of the experience. An event that is in itself traumatic, such as the early loss of a parent, or an accident, or a message delivered with great emotional power (anger, fear, sadness, etc.) can create the beginning of the chain by itself. The younger you are the easier it is for the event to feel traumatic (try taking a sweet from a child!) – this is because of the lack of experience with which to compare the present situation.

2 The frequency. An event or message, perhaps delivered with less intensity but often, such as 'You're stupid,' can cumulatively provide the effect.

3 The repetition. Similar to above, except that the power derives from the length of the period of exposure to the message rather than its frequency.

4 The individual threshold. Everybody has a different neurological capacity to handle the transmission of nerve messages to the mind. This may be why people have different stress thresholds – some have nervous systems that can handle the input of information more effectively than others.

This factor is the determinant of how intense, how frequent or how often an event or message has to be before it becomes a significant emotional event for that person.

Traditional talking therapies have focused on identifying such patterns. Some believe that understanding the pattern behind the problem will relieve the symptoms (in simple terms, the Freudian approach); others believe that reliving the events will cathartically release the negative emotions that generate the problem (as of many counselling approaches, as well as many traditional hypnotherapists). I believe that merely going back over a problem will only serve to reinforce it. Recall of a negative memory must be for the purpose of changing the client's perception of it (remember Epicetus on page 6).

MEMORY IS TOTAL

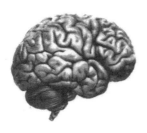

The constellation model gives an idea of the scale of our memory. Evidence supports the suggestion that our memory is total. Back in the 1950s a neuro-surgeon called Wilder Penfield performed a series of brain operations on conscious patients who suffered from epilepsy.

Part of the operation involved touching parts of the brain that deal with memory with a low voltage electronic probe. He found that touching a specific point on the brain brought to recall a specific memory for the patient.

Repeated touching of the same point recalled the same memory.

Not only was the event recalled, but the feelings that were associated at the time were reproduced. The patient felt again the emotion that the situation originally produced, and was aware of the same interpretations, true or false, that he or she gave to the experience in the first place.[10]

So the memory is not exactly like a video recording, it is the patient's version of the original event in terms of how it was seen, and heard, and felt, and understood, at that point in his or her life.

For example, if at an early age you saw your parents arguing, the memory of it is likely to be tinged with fear and anxiety and given a personal significance that it didn't have for your parents, and which you wouldn't give it now if you could magically time travel back and watch it as an adult.

Everyday events can act on us in a similar way to Dr Penfield's probe. Have you ever smelt something that suddenly whisks you to an earlier time (along the string of pearls)? Walk into a school canteen and smell the cabbage and all of a sudden you are back in short trousers or pigtails. This may last only a few seconds, or it may last a while, but as it lasts long forgotten feelings flood into your consciousness, making you feel happy or sad, angry or frightened.

The sequence of these unconscious recollections is:

1   Reliving (spontaneous, involuntary feelings)

and

2   Remembering (conscious awareness of the past event relived).

What this means is that we feel feelings from the past before we know the event that they relate to, and importantly much of what we relive we cannot remember (*background*) – it is not admitted to consciousness – so we feel something without knowing why. For example, you are at a party with a bunch of friends having a good time. You leave the group to get a drink. As you walk away they all suddenly burst out laughing. You feel a sudden flush in your cheeks and a pain inside you somewhere. A voice inside you says 'They're laughing at me!'

Now the likelihood is that someone just told a joke, but the incident has triggered a feeling from the past, probably of an occasion when you were young and felt you didn't 'belong'. The actual incident has been repressed by your unconscious so you probably cannot remember the actual incident, but you can relive both the feelings and the decision (belief) you made – 'I don't belong' – when some incident in the present triggers the wounded memory.

A little like an accountant, the unconscious presents you with the end result of its processing (a feeling) without showing you its working out, so you have no idea of its faulty calculation – you just remain a victim of it.

However, the conscious need to feel in executive control will usually result in any such unexplained feeling being rationalised: 'I feel like that because...', which will often extend the generalisation of that particular matrix, or even begin to generate a new one. An example might be someone who is suffering from panic attacks. They are usually triggered by something in the environment, or by an over-sensitivity to a bodily sensation, such as blushing or increased heart beat. Sometimes the response to a bodily sensation can be so subtle that the sufferer is completely unaware of the trigger for the panic attack. In that situation she will often rationalise it as being something to do with her environment at the moment it occurred. 'It happened in a supermarket, it must be something to do with that.' This belief makes it more likely that it will happen the next time she goes to a supermarket, so the anticipation adds a new strand to that matrix. Again, we are talking about our interpretation of events creating a 'belief'.

The writer Robert Anton Wilson suggests a dual mental mechanism of 'the thinker' and 'the prover'. He suggests that once the 'thinker' has developed a belief about any aspect of existence, the 'prover' will adjust the input from our senses to validate the belief. The maxim is 'What the thinker thinks, the prover proves.'[11] It is the basis for our self-fulfilling prophecies.

Sigmund Freud's daughter Anna did a lot of useful work on what she termed 'ego defence', which is the range of processes the unconscious uses to protect our self-image. For now I just want to concentrate on one defence used in the context of memory – repression. The unconscious tends to repress negative events so that they are not available for ordinary recall.

When clients come to you with a problem they will rarely be conscious of the series of events that has led to their condition. They might give recent examples, or give incidents from their childhood, but in my experience it is rare for them to know of the first event connected to the problem. The unconscious will either have repressed it, or deleted the emotional connection, so that although they remember the event they have no awareness of its significance to the problem.

Conventional wisdom (predominantly Freudian inspired conventional wisdom) supposes that such memories are buried deep in the psyche and take years of therapeutic digging to raise them to awareness. That might be because Freud abandoned hypnosis in favour of free association. My experience has been that such memories are held strongly in the memory and can be brought to consciousness using only a light trance state. My hypothesis for why this is so is based on this idea of the matrix.

As a metaphor, imagine the unconscious playing a game of snap. Behind the curtain of your awareness it has a collection (like a pack of cards) of hundreds of events that have emotional significance for you – both positive and negative. As you move through your day it is looking for any situation that is the same, or similar, to one of these cards. When it finds a match it shouts 'Snap!' and triggers you into reliving the feelings from that first event. As a consequence of those feelings the unconscious then runs whatever defensive behaviour is connected with it if it is a negative match (as with Mrs Toothbrush, a panic attack or gag response). In the case of a positive match the feelings experienced are likely to be confidence, competence, relaxing, excitement, anticipation etc.

Unfortunately not many clients come complaining about feeling competent, so my emphasis will continue to be on thought processes with negative outcomes.

The purpose of my approach, and the goal of Wordweaving,™ is to disrupt or change the process or structure of any matrix that leads to a negative outcome. It does so by reprocessing the meaning of past events to change the algorithmic connection from 'This is the same as that' or 'This is because of that' to 'This [present situation or event] is not the same as that [past event].'

I intend to cover the regression techniques used to identify the initial sensitising event and how to reprocess the meaning in my next book. This volume is going to concentrate on suggestions aimed at the other points of the Matrix Model that can be used to alter what the client's 'thinker' thinks. Because effecting a change in any part of the Matrix Model will affect the whole of the model, suggestions that change a client's perception of the stimulus, emotion, response, termination or evaluation will have an effect on the power of the memory matrix to hijack behaviour, by linking such changes in perception to a change in belief.

Neuro-logical Levels

The relationship between identity and beliefs, and then their relationship to our abilities and behaviour is usefully described by a model that one of NLP's most original thinkers, Robert Dilts, created from work initiated by Gregory Bateson, which Dilts calls 'Neuro-logical Levels'.[12] I think it is one of the most useful, and least used, models in NLP, and is central to Wordweaving.™

Bateson suggested that the brain, in fact any biological or social system, is organised into levels.[13] We all operate at different levels of thinking and being at different moments in time. My version of Dilts' model assumes five levels of operation.

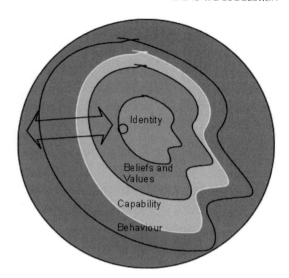

Fig 3 Neuro-logical Levels

The basic level of operation is our environment, the external constraints we work within. We operate on that environment through our behaviour, the second level. Our behaviour is guided by our mental maps and our strategies, which define our capabilities, the third level. These capabilities are organised by belief systems and values, the fourth level, and these are organised by our identity, the fifth level. In the way I have drawn the Neuro-logical Levels in Figure 3 I wanted to represent the way the different levels emanate from the core level of identity, though the ripples run both ways. I also want to make the point that the body can form part of the environment. For example, with people with anxiety conditions it is often something physiological, like a surge in heart rate, that triggers the panic attack. In that context the surge within the body is at the level of environment.

The brilliant psychotherapist Stephen Wolinsky has suggested that we develop what he calls trance identities; that at those times when we are in the grip of emotional hijacking we have a distinct and separate version of our personality that controls our actions. If we link the model of Neuro-logical Levels to this idea of 'trance identities'[14] we can say that each identity will have beliefs that limit them, which will generate a perception of a lack of capabilities, which will produce behaviour that supports the identity (such as a person who has a belief 'I'm stupid' who seizes up before an exam).

The environment will often be the trigger for the emergence of this trance identity, as it provides the context for the behaviour (in this case an exam room). In Figure 4 you can see how this then connects with the Matrix Model:

> Each trance identity a person has is generated from a memory matrix that forms in response to the emotional meaning the memories are given.

> These meanings are expressed as beliefs, such as 'I'm a loser,' 'I'm stupid,' 'I deserve to be punished.'

> In response to these beliefs we will develop values around what is important to us, and what is not. These values will motivate us to act, or not to act, as the case may be.

Our capabilities in situations controlled by a trance identity are likely to be limited. For instance I used to have a trance identity generated by DIY. The thought of doing anything practical would generate a 'belief' that 'It will go wrong, it always does' (inevitability). This gave rise to the limitations I felt I had about my practical skills (capabilities), which led to avoidance behaviour whenever I could get away with it. When I couldn't avoid it, the post-hypnotic suggestion inherent in my belief nearly always came true – and I lived in an environment with no shelves!

Within Neuro-logical Levels each level organises the levels below it, so in therapy the higher the level you influence the

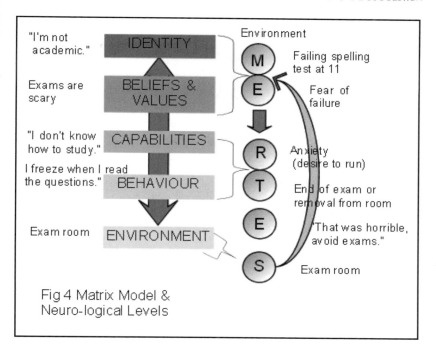

"I'm not academic."

Exams are scary

"I don't know how to study."

I freeze when I read the questions."

Exam room

IDENTITY

BELIEFS & VALUES

CAPABILITIES

BEHAVIOUR

ENVIRONMENT

Environment

M

E

R

T

E

S

Failing spelling test at 11

Fear of failure

Anxiety (desire to run)

End of exam or removal from room

"That was horrible, avoid exams."

Exam room

Fig 4 Matrix Model & Neuro-logical Levels

more profound the effect you are likely to have. The same is often true of the Matrix Model. This might be why behaviourist approaches take so long to have an effect – they are at too low a level – and why some NLP interventions that are working at the behavioural level often bring only a temporary improvement.

If we use Mrs Toothbrush as an example we can see that the toothbrush acts as the stimulus (environment). Her memory matrix generates fear in response to the incident at eighteen months. Her belief is 'I'm scared of toothbrushes.' This affects her capabilities – she cannot clean her teeth and feels unable to go to the dentist. Her behaviour is to avoid the proximity of the toothbrush.

Let us look more closely at Neuro-logical Levels.

IDENTITY

At this level we function as a 'self', a self-organising entity that we observe as being consistent over time. Our identity is that part of us we consider the 'I'.

BELIEFS

Beliefs organise our model of the world. They are key constellations in our personal universe. If you believe that you are a competent, confident human being your life will unfold in a completely different way from a person living your life but believing she is inferior and incompetent.

Beliefs lie at the heart of our behaviour, and serve to give meaning to our life. They are the material from which our trance identities emerge. We all have a set of core beliefs that can be highly predictive of our performance over time, and can lead to unconscious inevitabilities:

> ➢ Behavioural inevitabilities made up of beliefs that, for example, 'I always get that wrong,' and which lead to behaviour that fulfils such a prophecy.

> ➢ Emotional inevitabilities, such as 'Every time I let someone close they hurt me.' Again, behaviour is manifested that creates this repeatedly, such as the kind of clinging insecurity that drives the other person away.

> ➢ Lifestyle inevitabilities generated by a belief that 'I haven't got what it takes to be a success,' which leads to remaining stuck in a poorly paid job because to do otherwise risks disaster.

> ➢ C>E inevitabilities, which presuppose apparent destiny, such as 'I'm an unlucky person, that's why it all goes wrong,' or 'I'll never get a girl because I'm ugly.'

The power that beliefs have is immense because they are not based on reality. In fact they replace knowledge about reality, which is why environmental and behavioural evidence to the contrary alone will not change them. That understanding is vital if suggestions are to have the desired effect.

A classic story from abnormal psychology illustrates the point. A patient believes he is a corpse. He doesn't eat or work, he just sits around claiming to be a corpse. The psychiatrist tries to convince him that he is not a corpse by saying, 'Do corpses bleed?'

The patient thinks about that and says, 'No, all body functions have shut down so they wouldn't bleed.' So the psychiatrist pricks him with a needle and the man starts to bleed. The patient looks amazed, and exclaims, 'I'll be damned, corpses do bleed!'

Trying to talk about the existence of God to a believer is another example. People filter facts through their beliefs. It is the facts that will usually get distorted as a result, not the beliefs. Ultimately suggestions must be geared towards changing the client's beliefs.

DEFINITION OF BELIEFS

Robert Dilts defined beliefs as generalisations around three categories,[15] the first two of which mirror the algorithms we use to describe how the mind sorts information, cause and effect (this is because of that), or A = B (complex equivalence; this means, or is the same as, that):

1 CAUSE AND EFFECT GENERALISATIONS (C > E)

For example:

> ➤ What do you believe causes the increasing rate of divorce?

> ➤ People meet too many people these days.

> ➢ Divorce is too easy.

> ➢ People don't go to church anymore.

> ➢ Men can't commit or women are all nags.

Your beliefs in this area will determine how you cope with the prospect of divorce, what you do to avoid it, whom you blame. If you believe that divorce is wrong it will make a difference in how you treat its possibility, as will believing it is an inevitable consequence of modern living. Who do you think is going to try the hardest to keep the relationship going?

2 GENERALISATION ABOUT MEANING RELATIONSHIPS (A = B)

For example, if you get divorced what does it mean?

> ➢ That you were in some way inadequate?

> ➢ That your partner is slime and deserves to die?

> ➢ That you hate yourself?

> ➢ That it is an opportunity to create a completely new life with wonderful opportunities?

The meaning will determine how you respond.

3 GENERALISATIONS ABOUT LIMITS

You can believe that you will put up with a certain behaviour to a certain level but no further. You believe that you can do something to a certain level of competence, but no further. You believe that someone can be trusted to a certain degree, but no further.

TYPES OF BELIEF ISSUES

There are typically three types of belief issues that arise from these generalisations:

Hopelessness

If a person is hopeless he feels an outcome is just not possible. This is a belief about the outcome. If it is just not possible why even try? An example would be 'Nobody gets over AIDS, so why bother?'

Helplessness

'I am not able to do that, other people can, but I can't.'

Worthlessness

People won't try to do something they don't believe they deserve, or will sabotage their effort in order to get the payoff: 'Well, I didn't really deserve it, other people needed it more than I did.'

> Remember: you can spend your life
> exploring either your limitations, or
> your possibilities. Which are you
> doing? Houdini was right when he said,
> 'All limitations are illusions.'

Values

Richard Bandler has said that

'Values are the thing that get us out of bed in the morning.'

They provide motivation for what we do, and after-the-fact evaluation of our performance. If you put a high value on money your career is likely to be different from someone's who values fun. If you don't think that education is important you won't put much energy into study.

CAPABILITY

This level comprises our skills and abilities. It contains all those things that define our competence to ourselves, or lack of.

BEHAVIOUR

Our behaviour is the level at which we interact with the world.

ENVIRONMENT

As stated earlier our environment is everything that is not our neurology (let's not go into the idea that there is nothing except our neurology). That includes our body and the world outside our skin.

In most cases a Neuro-logical Level will be responsible for each point of the Matrix Model process. In a way the Neuro-logical Levels are the drivers of each point of the process: if nothing was identified in the environment there would be no stimulus; if there was no negative belief there would be no need for a response etc.

Neuro-logical Levels extend those elements of the client that we can aim our suggestions at. So we can become more specific about the first step of Wordweaving™ by saying:

Your objective in the first step of
Wordweaving™ is to aim each
suggestion at a particular point of the
Matrix Model, or at one of the Neuro-
logical Levels, in order to adapt the
client's perception of that point or
level.

So far we have explored stimulus and memory. Let's continue
through the Matrix Model to see where else we can aim our
suggestions.

Emotion – its role and structure

It might be useful to generalise between two
different functions that emotions/feelings
have:

- Evaluation
- Protection

EVALUATION

Evaluation is a cognitive function that is active rather than
reactive. It assesses options and choices, works out plans and
makes decisions. It involves being aware of consequences,
which implies the ability to construct the future. As far as
we know it is restricted to organisms that are conscious.

To show how feelings are used for evaluation let me tell
you the tale of Elliott.

Elliott had an operation to remove a fast-growing tumour
from an area near the front of his brain. A large chunk of tissue
surrounding the tumour was lost in the process, and with it

went Elliott's ability to feel emotion. Observers noted that Elliott was always controlled. He described events as a dispassionate onlooker, however horrific those events, and had no sense of his own suffering. It was a life without love, joy, anger, or guilt. You might think this existence to be dull, but you might also expect it to have some advantages. After all, isn't a 'calm head' meant to be best to solve problems and make rational decisions?

In fact the opposite proved to be true. Elliott's IQ remained the same, his memory was fine, and his powers of deduction were unaffected. Yet he found it hard to make the simplest decision. Faced with a problem, he could generate a range of appropriate responses, but he could not distinguish which was the best one. No one response felt any more right than another. He had lost his 'gut instincts'. In the end he went bankrupt because he threw himself into enterprises that to everyone else were obviously dodgy, and picked totally untrustworthy business partners.

It is by our feelings that we *know*; it is the interaction between our emotional system and the frontal cortex. The story demonstrates how our perceptions and behaviour are informed by brain processes of which we are often not conscious, but that are registered physically in the body. Truly the mind and the body do communicate.

As Rita Carter states in *Mapping the Mind*:

'Without feedback from our bodies emotions are indistinguishable from thoughts.'

Research on people with high spinal injuries who cannot feel anything below the neck typically reports a damping down of emotion. One such patient explained:

'Sometimes I act angry when I see some injustice, I yell and curse and raise hell because if you don't do it sometimes I have learned people take advantage of you. But it doesn't have the heat it used to [before the injury].'[16]

Our emotional vocabulary – the 'aching heart', the 'lump in the throat', and the 'pain in the neck' – are kinaesthetic words that reflect the direct connection between body states and felt emotion. I hope you can see the nature of the mind-body loop – that damage to the brain prevents us from feeling emotion; damage to the body has the same effect. Emotion is not the preserve of either, it is a product of the connection between them, and a language with which the mind and body communicate.

This connection is vital in understanding the nature of people's problems. Our use of feelings to evaluate our thoughts can also mean that where we have a feeling we will seek to explain it, usually by the algorithm C>E (this is because of that). It can lead to situations where objects are connected with a strong emotion because of their proximity at the moment the emotion was experienced (a distortion).

To take an example, an eighteen-stone police officer came to see me with a powerful spider phobia. The first event connected to the fear was at the age of five, when his father was reading him a story in bed. At the end of the story the boy pulled back his bedcovers and saw a spider sitting on the blanket. It made him jump so much he stood up on the bed. His father laughed at him and the boy felt stupid and ashamed. Unconsciously the spider became linked with those feelings. It is as if the unconscious says to itself, 'These feelings are bad, what can I do to keep them from happening again? Well, what caused it [looks around]? The spider. So, if I keep you away from spiders in future you will no longer get those feelings.'

Because fear is the physiological trigger to move us away from something threatening, the man feels fear whenever he sees a spider, simply to get him away from it. Sound logic for a five-year-old, but not appropriate now.

This 'premature evaluation' by our immature thinking is the root of most of the problems we have.

The Swiss educationalist Jean Piaget studied the cognitive development of hundreds of children of various ages. One of his areas of interest was their ability to process and understand information of varying degrees of complexity. He gave children reasoning problems in order to observe how they manipulated the information to reach their conclusion.[17]

For example, if children below the age of seven are shown a photo of two trees differing in type and height, they will choose the tall tree as being the older. Children older than about seven will tend to ask when the trees were planted. In other words, the older children have the ability to take more information into account when reasoning.

The different levels of cognitive complexity that develop in children as they mature can be broken into four. These categories are 'nominal', 'ordinal', 'interval' and 'ratio'.

NOMINAL DATA

Nominal data is processed in all-or-nothing terms. Things are either good or bad, right or wrong, winning or losing. This level of processing admits no grey areas. It can be identified in speech when people are saying things like 'You're either with me or against me.'

This level of thinking frequently accompanies limiting beliefs and decisions. Young children cannot escape this style of thinking owing to their cognitive limitations, and this is why most problems adults face through feeling inadequate, or not worthwhile, or unloved, have their root in this phase of life. The primary event in most memory matrices you deal with will be before the age of twelve, principally because of nominal processing, or 'premature evaluation', as I label it (and yes, I've heard all the jokes!).

What you will normally find is that when adults are in the grip of emotional stress they regress to this mode of thinking. It is why you can rationalise with a person who is angry, jealous or scared until the cows come home, but it is like talking to a brick wall. He will be stuck in simplistic thought patterns, unable to see things differently until the emotions subside. As Joseph LeDoux likes to say,

'Strong emotions make us stupid.'[18]

ORDINAL PROCESSING

This second category provides a way of ranking information in terms of the increase or decrease of some quality of that information. It involves comparison in order to generate an order or rank. For example, in a race children receive information about where they are placed, as in 'I came second,' rather than just the 'nominal' calculation 'I won' or 'I lost.' You can see that this is a slightly more sophisticated level of processing than nominal, but children making decisions about themselves using ordinal processing are still likely to make major errors.

INTERVAL PROCESSING

Interval processing adds more sophistication than the previous two levels through more abstraction, as in being able to take into account the degrees in a relationship, such as by how much I was beaten in a race, not just that I was beaten; how close I came to winning, not just that I came second.

RATIO PROCESSING

Finally, ratio processing represents the most sophisticated level of thought. It contains all of the previous three levels but also allows for more abstract considerations such as 'does winning actually matter?' It is usually what we are referring to when we talk about 'thinking out of the box'. It is where we are not restricted to our usual thinking pattern. It is the processing to seek in our clients when we assist them to look at a problem from a different perceptual position.

Our ability to think at these different levels of processing develops over time in the course of our maturity. Piaget's research showed that children are limited to nominal and ordinal processing until roughly the age seven, and then develop interval and ratio processing through the ages of eight to twelve. However, when in the grip of strong emotions, adults will still tend to slip back into nominal processing.

So, the beliefs we form about ourselves when we are children are limited by our cognitive capacity. They represent the best we could do at the time. The point of Wordweaving™ is to cause our clients to undo beliefs based on their nominal phase, and enable them to create new beliefs *now*, when they can be stimulated to use ratio processing and the full range of their cognitive abilities.

PROTECTION

Protection in this sense is the reactive function that has evolved over millions of years, the feeling that motivates us to act. We know it principally by the action of the 'fight or flight' mechanism.

In the view of evolutionary psychology we are programmed for survival. It is the sole purpose of evolution to adapt us in order for us to pass our genes from one generation to the next. At this level our unconscious is geared to move us towards pleasure and away from pain or danger. In most creatures this is a very simple mechanism and is easily demonstrated by making your dog jump, and then stroking it.

In humans it has become more complicated because of our ability to evaluate, so sometimes we deliberately seek fear in order to fulfil something else that is important to what Freud might term our 'ego', and which others call our 'self'. We no longer have to worry about physical survival alone, but also social survival. In circumstances where the former is not an issue, or where we feel we can control the risk, we may undertake behaviour that is calculated to improve such concepts as self-respect or self-confidence – or simply to manipulate our hormone system in order to get an adrenaline or endorphin rush. It forms the basis of many active hobbies.

Many researchers have sought to number our emotions. I read one account that suggested we have over seventy. From a therapy point of view the precise number, and the names given to them, are not too important. The name given to an emotion by your clients when they experience their problem is more important than whether it matches what researchers have called it.

I think it is possible to look at the types of feelings we experience, like jealousy, envy, guilt, etc., and classify them by their function, i.e. what they are for.

The 'primary emotions' function as physical protection, and the 'process emotions' function as the protection of our 'social self'. Primary emotions are those that have evolved over millions of years to protect us. They are part of a chemical system designed to elicit a response in us without the need for thought. I think there are three primary emotions:

> Fear (to get us to freeze or run)

> Anger (to get us to defend ourselves)

> Pleasure/love (to encourage us to repeat the positive activity).

Each has a positive survival value, and it is as a result of only extreme trauma, or premature evaluation, that they impact negatively on our lives. We will look now at how this can occur.

EMOTIONAL HIJACKING

This is crucial to understand. I often say to clients that you can think or feel but not at the same time. By this I mean that the evolution of the brain means that the limbic system – our emotional mind – if triggered beyond a certain threshold can inhibit the higher functions of the brain. The consequence of this is that while in its grip we are less than human. Daniel Goleman in his book *Emotional Intelligence* says:

> 'In the dance of feelings and thought the emotional faculty guides our moment-to-moment decisions, working hand in hand with the rational mind, enabling – or disabling – thought itself. Likewise, the thinking brain plays an executive role in our emotions – except in those moments when emotions surge out of control and the emotional mind runs rampant.'[19]

When it runs rampant it effectively puts us in a trance state where our focus narrows. We become stupid. Think of somebody in a fit of jealousy. He cannot be talked to. He continues to loop through the same thoughts and is certain of his own viewpoint. All he will hear is what confirms his own thoughts (nominal processing). Emotional arousal beyond a certain point inhibits people's ability to think. This means they cannot process information accurately.

People don't tend to think 'I'm panicking!' They just 'do' panic, and afterwards think 'I panicked!' With *primary* responses what happens is this: information flows from the senses to the thalamus, which looks to match it with information already interpreted and stored in the brain (matrix matching). Part of any such matching is likely to be by referring to the part of the brain called the amygdala, which has the job of deciding the emotional significance of the information and how to respond. It is particularly involved in fear and anger responses.

If matrix response is below threshold (i.e. it does not contain an SEE (SEE)), the signals from the senses pass through different parts of the brain to the cortex and are formed into a thought that is available to the conscious mind.

If the matrix contains an SEE, then this processing is interrupted and the amygdala triggers the fight or flight system, and we become 'emotionally hijacked' until the situation is resolved.

The problem with the primary emotions is that the evolutionary responses are basic (nominal). If we feel anger or fear (which are obviously stresses) our body responds with the 'sympathetic' system pumping adrenaline and allied hormones round our bodies. At a low level of arousal we become aware of 'butterflies' in the stomach – that is blood leaving the area and moving into our arms and legs to prepare us to fight or run. The increased blood pressure is why we shake. If the unconscious perception continues then we might start to sweat – because muscles work better if they are warm. Our breathing might become faster – because the more oxygen in the bloodstream the better. At a certain level blood will be diverted from the cortex – because we don't need to think in order to fight or run, in fact too much thinking might inhibit our responses.

This system has been of evolutionary benefit for ninety-nine per cent of the existence of the human race. The problem may be that we have mentally and socially advanced in the last one per cent more quickly than we have physically evolved to compensate. This sympathetic response clearly assisted us against sabre-toothed tigers, not with job interviews, divorce, or redundancy. Nowadays, with the stresses of modern life that provoke fear and anger, this response can actually be counterproductive.

For example, if you have a memory matrix that has led to a fear of exams, then the physical symptoms you experience are simply your unconscious recognising the stress to your system that 'exam equals threat' $(A = B)$ has elicited, and is preparing

45

you to fight or run away from it. The more you resist this impulse the stronger it becomes. 'Hey presto' – a panic attack – and it is just the unconscious trying to help. Of course, you won't be aware of the structure of the matrix that causes the fear. Your conscious part will simply have the verbalised belief 'I don't like exams, I'm no good at exams, I'm stupid, thick, useless,' etc.

If our stress level remains raised over a length of time it places a strain on the immune system. The chemicals that we experience as 'stress' (adrenaline, cortisol etc.) can have a damaging effect on the organs of the body if they are subjected to them for too long. The immune system scavenges them out of the blood stream. If it is required to do this on a constant basis it tires and cannot cope with performing the many tasks required of it – such as fighting infection. That is why people under prolonged stress begin to succumb to illness – the immune system simply cannot cope with the demands placed on it.

In summary, primary-emotion responses are the direct result of 10,000,000 years of evolution adapting us to face physical threat (anger and fear), and motivating us to seek out activities that promote gene survival (attraction and love). They still work to our benefit on many occasions, such as getting out of the way of a speeding car, or running away from a crowd of yobs, or meeting your soul mate.

Most problems arise when the matrix-matching abilities of the brain are still immature, and so cause-and-effect mistakes are easily made. We are creatures who seek meaning. Nothing is allowed just 'to happen'. So even from the earliest age we are looking to make sense of the world, to make it predictable. Cognitive psychology suggests that we act as scientists, forming personal hypotheses about the way the world works, and creating behaviour that is appropriate to these beliefs.

Add to the idea of the thinker and prover the presupposition that the unconscious acts as a protective device, using previous events in our life to determine appropriate action in the present, and we have a recipe for premature evaluation. An easy illustration of this is through describing a phobia using these presuppositions.

A man came to see me with a fear of fish. He couldn't even watch the Goldfish credit-card advert on TV. Using cognitive hypnotherapy I regressed him to the first event connected to his problem. He recalled a time when he was three when his father came home early in the morning from a night sea fishing. As some fathers do he thought it would be funny to make his son jump, so he put his catch (which sounded like a conger eel) on his son's bed. The little boy felt the weight of it and opened his eyes – to find the face of the eel inches from his. As you can imagine, it scared the life out of him.

Now, working with the assumptions I began with, his unconscious needs to protect him from any similar 'dangerous' occasions. At that age, as Piaget demonstrated, a child's logical ability is limited to nominal processing.

Using this level of sophistication the unconscious searches for black and white causation. 'What has caused this fear? It must be the fish. If I keep you away from fish you will be safe.' Thus, this significant emotional event acts as a reference point for the unconscious to measure such threats in the future. Every time he comes into contact with a fish, or anticipates doing so, his unconscious prompts the fight or flight response into action, to get him away from the danger (or to kill it). Because this event is stored unconsciously – is an SEE, and so gets 'hijacked' by the amygdala – he is not aware of this mental computation, only of the result, which is an overwhelming emotional response: proximity to fish causes what he describes as a 'panic attack'. The intention is to protect him. The result is to restrict his life inappropriately. Remember, I said the unconscious is there to protect you, not necessarily to make you happy.

Every time he confronts a fish, and emerges unscathed because of his response, his response is reinforced (what the thinker thinks). The matrix around this context continues to be strengthened as time goes on.

Overwhelmingly, irrespective of what problem presents itself, the SEE that began the matrix that caused the problem happens below the age of twelve, when the brain is still developing the ability to rationalise in shades of grey. If Mr Fish had the first scary event at thirty, when his girlfriend leaves a fish in his bed, he might jump out of his skin, and probably call her some choice names, but he wouldn't develop a fish phobia, because his unconscious can make an evaluation from a much broader range of information than was available to him when he was three.

Process emotions – protecting our 'self'

So we have an emotional system within the mind whose purpose it is to protect us from physical harm. During the course of evolution we have also developed the ability to think. This enables us to build amazingly complicated models of how the world works. Being 'conscious' also allows us to observe ourselves within this world, particularly our social world, an ability apparently unique to humans.

The interaction between our thinking brain and our emotional brain has led us to use emotions to evaluate our place in the world in order to keep us safe within the society we inhabit. Evolutionary psychology suggests that our mind has developed specific mental modules to deal with specific survival problems.[20] Beside the survival problems below I have appended what may be the negative consequences of what evolved as things that help us survive. The most important survival issues were thought to be:

> Avoiding predators – *phobias.*
> Eating the right food – *eating disorders, weight problems.*

> Forming alliances and friendships – *low self-esteem, jealousy, insecurity.*

> Providing help to children and other relatives – *guilt.*

> Reading other people's minds – *paranoia.*

> Communicating with other people – *alienation, social phobias.*

> Selecting mates – jealousy, insecurity, *possessiveness.*

You can see that all but two of them are to do with social interaction, which shows that the importance of 'how we get on within the group' has been consistent over millions of years. You could argue that the module we call 'I', our 'self', has the purpose of monitoring how we are 'getting on' with others, and that behaviour is generated (still according to the pleasure principle) that keeps us away from anything – people, activities, or situations – that threatens our social status, and rewards us for anything that improves it. (In my opinion this is the root of what is wrong with our consumer culture, because it preys on and encourages our insecurity.) It is possible that these modules, now working in an environment that they did not evolve for, produce the negative self-assessment that drives low self-esteem.

Our first social need is a uniquely intimate and vulnerable one. From the moment of our birth we are imprinted with the need to form attachment to our parents, because the evolutionary lesson has been that 'children who bond with their parents will be nurtured and survive, and those that do not will be abandoned and die.' Consequently we are acutely tuned to the responses of our parents towards us. It is an area uniquely ripe for premature evaluation around the issue of 'I am loved/I am not loved.' One of the greatest of all hypnotherapists, Gil Boyne, asserts that 'the basis of a client's presenting problem will always be a feeling of being unloved or unlovable.'[21]

In his view there is only one phobia – fear of being unlovable. Once this belief has been formed it will tend to be mapped into other areas of social interaction. Acting on the pleasure principle, we develop matrix behaviours that make us feel loved, and matrix behaviours that take us away from feeling 'not loved'. These behaviours are many and infinitely varied. You will see an amazing variety of client behaviours that ultimately boil down to this issue. I agree with Gil Boyne that 'I am not loved/lovable' could be described as the universal human neurosis, because almost nobody gets through childhood without feeling unloved at some point, and it is a feeling that more completely causes an SEE than just about any other. You will identify it time and again in your clients.

As a belief that lies at the core of your world matrix, 'I'm not loved/lovable/wanted' will influence you in all your relationships with others, and will cause you to perceive their responses to you in a certain way. The pleasure principle will drive you away from any activity that activates the belief.

As a generalisation, process emotions are involved with our social survival, whereas our primary emotions are involved with physical survival. Our bodily response, however, tends to be the same (move towards it if it's good, run or destroy it if it's bad).

If our social survival becomes too difficult, by loss of a job, rejection by a partner etc. then our emotional response may reach its threshold. In those circumstances primary fight-or-flight responses (anger and fear) are likely to be activated by a process issue (jealousy, guilt, insecurity), causing panic attacks, anxiety, depression or violence.

The concept of social survival returns us to the concept of 'self', the unique sense of ourselves that we have, and of our position in the world or universe. It is the part that Tor Norretranders in his book *The User Illusion* calls the 'I' (the conscious identity), in contrast to the 'me' (the unconscious identity). He quotes James Clerk Maxwell, who unified the forces of electricity and magnetism with his elegant equations,

'What is done by what is called myself is, I feel, done by something greater than myself in me.'[22]

Process emotions are those feelings we have about ourselves (our 'I') in relation to our 'okay-ness', and the rules we have about the behaviour of ourselves and others.

Thus, emotions such as jealousy, sadness, guilt, frustration and inadequacy are labels given to feelings we have in relation to others. I include how we feel about ourselves in how we feel in relation to others. For example, a feeling of inadequacy might trigger the emotion of fear in relation to particular contexts, such as public speaking, so that the person will have a panic attack in response to having to stand up in front of people.

In most people response to process emotions is less dramatic. The person's personality and behaviour become subtly shaped over time by the unconscious pressure of the pleasure principle. The feelings will generally be experienced only as a 'lack of confidence', or 'shyness'. Veering away from certain behaviours will be rationalised by the consciousness as 'I don't like doing those things,' or 'I'm not very good at that.' If you have ever watched someone doing something that you secretly long to do but 'just can't', you are probably in the grip of a process emotion.

Cognitive therapy seeks to have the client identify the automatic thoughts that these emotions generate, such as 'I'm not very good at that,' and then use the client's interval and ratio processing to question and re-evaluate the thought. In cognitive hypnotherapy we seek to identify the primary or process emotion matrix that generates the automatic thought, and change it. The hypnotic suggestions to be made are intended to disrupt the Matrix Model process that brings those thoughts into life. If the external event that triggers the problem can be construed differently as it is experienced, then the underlying limitation would never spring into life, and over time would wither away or be re-evaluated.

To hammer it home once more – in both primary and process situations the trigger for a response will be the consequence of the matrices that the individual has developed during his or her life. They can be changed. Any feeling is available to re-interpretation, for after all we use feelings to evaluate the meaning of what is happening to us. If you are enjoying a roller-coaster ride you would probably label the feeling fun or excitement. A moment later, as you hear the bolt shear under your seat, that feeling, which is probably the same chemically, will be given a different name. At some stage of a hypnotic session it is likely that part of the purpose of your suggestions will be to adjust the meaning of a feeling connected to the client's problem.

Response

Depending on the emotions and their strength, a thought sequence and/or a behaviour result. In Neuro-logical Levels response corresponds to the level of behaviour. There is an infinite variety of behaviours generated by people. I am constantly amazed at the way that people with the same root cause of a problem manifest it in such a range of ways. It is one of the things that makes therapy so fascinating. Three people might present with a lack of confidence. The first has an SEE from three years old, when her parents brought home a baby brother; the second has an SEE at seven, when a teacher humiliated her in front of the class; and the third is affected by his parents' divorce when he was nine.

Put another way, three clients each have as core issue 'I'm not lovable.' One presents with a history of broken relationships, one with an unspecified feeling of depression, and the third binge eats. The beauty of this model is that it allows for the infinite creative capacity of the mind to cause problems, but has a flexible framework with which to identify and track its development.

A model that explains this variety of effect comes from a new branch of science called Chaos Theory, which examines the workings of complex systems like the action of gases, the weather – and the brain. The popular name for the model is the 'Butterfly Effect', and was discovered by Edward Lorenz, a meteorologist working on the prediction of weather systems. He created a computer program to simulate weather conditions. Through it he could type in a series of numbers that represented variables such as wind direction, temperature and tide, and then allow the computer to develop the weather patterns that arise from these conditions.

The computer the program ran on had neither the speed nor memory to manage a realistic simulation of the earth's atmosphere and oceans, but it did seem to mimic many of the major principles. Lorenz had an intuition that weather repeated itself, a form of feedback loop, displaying familiar patterns over time – like pressure rising and falling, the air stream swinging from north to south. He found this to be true, but the repetitions were never quite exact. There was pattern with disturbances – a sort of orderly disorder.

His breakthrough came by accident, when the limitations of the computer caused a weather simulation to behave oddly. The simulation was a repeat of a previous experiment using exactly the same data, and yet he found the weather that the data produced diverged so rapidly from the pattern of the first run that, within a short space of time, all resemblance had disappeared. What had happened was that the computer's memory stored six decimal places (.506127). To save time on the second run Lorenz had entered only three (.506). He had assumed that the difference – 1 part in 1,000 – was inconsequential, as it represented the equivalent of a belch in a thunderstorm. It was a reasonable assumption, for surely the small parts faded or cancelled each other out before they could change important, large-scale features of the weather. Yet in Lorenz's system, small differences proved catastrophic.

His discovery was an accident that challenged an assumption that had been at the philosophical heart of science since the days of Newton. As one lecturer liked to tell his students:

> 'The basic idea of Western science is that you don't have to take into account the falling of a leaf on some planet in another galaxy when you're trying to account for the motion of a billiard ball on a pool table on earth. Very small influences can be neglected. There is a convergence in the way things work, and arbitrarily small influences don't blow up to have arbitrarily large effects.'

The Butterfly Effect showed that they do, that the flapping of the wings of a butterfly in Brazil could, somewhere down the line, be the beginning of a storm in Australia.

The technical name for the Butterfly Effect is 'sensitive dependence on initial conditions'.[23] It is relevant to therapy because brains use feedback loops to make sense of the world. Our mind/body system is one massive feedback loop.

As has been mentioned before, the reason why you recognise a chair is that you have seen one before. Variations on the theme of 'chair' are fed back into the brain to build a greater capacity for recognition. The reason why your body sends clotting agents to the site of a wound is due to information received from the skin cells. When it stops doing so this is the result of further information from those cells. In other words, another feedback loop. If we take this idea of sensitivity to initial conditions and relate it to the ideas of SEEs and the matrix structure of memory, we can see how people build a problem pattern that is totally unique to them, even though they are using thought patterns we all share.

In the case of therapy the 'butterfly' is the first SEE. That sets the framing context, the initial conditions. Conceivably two people could have the same event happen on the same day in the same way and give it the same meaning (though even that is unlikely). However, the odds against their having another event that their unconscious references to the first, on the same day, in the same way, are astronomical, and even higher for the subsequent events that form their particular matrix.

As time goes on, just as with Lorenz's experiment, a completely different pattern will emerge from the same initial conditions. It is like two boats heading out to sea from the same place at the same time. By accident one boat sets a course that is a tenth of a degree different from the other. Initially they will sail side by side, the difference indistinguishable. Weeks later they will be hundreds of miles apart.

Assuming the memory matrix to be a dynamic system within the brain, which exists and springs to life when activated by a present event, the butterfly effect gives us the reason why redefining a past event, or changing its $A = B$ or $C > E$ connection to a present situation, will change the client response to it in the present.

If you go back to the initial conditioning event, the first SEE, and change the perception and meaning of that event, then, because it acts as a reference for every subsequent event within its matrix, it must change the meaning of those as well. Because these events are the trigger for the present behaviour, the behaviour will also change. And, just as with a weather system, the behaviour will continue to change over time. It can never be the same again. Any small shift in the initial conditions can cause a major shift further down the line. Any change anywhere within the matrix will cause a shift that could be major at some point in the future.

It is why, very often, the SEE turns out to be a trivial event compared to the impact the consequence has on the person in the present. It is why, very often also, people report that the changes in them become more noticeable the more time goes on.

Regressive techniques can accomplish this, as can suggestions that change the perception of current information, so that no match is made to an SEE within the problem matrix. Ultimately the purpose of any hypnotic suggestion you make is the same – to make a disturbance within the client's problem matrix that will change its pattern for the better. Soon I will show you precisely how.

Termination

The exiting of that behaviour or thought sequence.

In a situation where emotional hijacking has taken place the behaviour will continue until the trigger is no longer present (you have moved away from or killed the stimulus). At that point the para-sympathetic system will activate and release endorphins into the body in order to calm it down. Behaviour will normalise, and full cognitive functioning will return.

If exposure to a stimulus is continuous then eventually the para-sympathetic system must activate. The body cannot maintain a peak state like panic indefinitely. We tend to label this event 'nervous exhaustion'. The same thing will eventually happen if the person is in a heightened state of excitation over a long period of time, but somewhere below threshold (we call it stress). The end result of an extended period of stress, particularly where the sufferer does not feel in control of what is causing the stress, is often depression.

Evaluation

A cognitive appraisal of the matrix sequence that confirms or denies its usefulness and validity.

All Matrix Model sequences are intended to protect the individual. At the end of such a sequence

it will be unconsciously evaluated in terms of whether it ful-
filled its original intention.

Mr Scared hates public speaking, because of a matrix that
began when his teacher ridiculed him in front of the class for
reading badly. He is best man at his friend's wedding. For weeks
prior to the event he is anxious as he contemplates the disaster
that is soon to occur. On the day he is a wreck as he struggles
against the fight or flight syndrome. He is in a no-win situation.

Scenario one

He wins the struggle and gets to stand up and give
his speech. His mind goes blank, he stutters and
stammers his way through a dreadfully delivered speech to
polite laughter. Post-event evaluation will be, 'You see, it was
a bloody disaster, I must keep away from that kind of thing.'
The next time anything of a similar nature occurs the
unconscious will work even harder to keep him away from it
until threshold is reached and he has a panic attack.

Scenario two

He loses the struggle and has a panic attack before
the speech and hides in the toilet, where he faints
or vomits. His conscious evaluation will be, 'You see what
happens if I try – I just don't have the confidence,' while his
unconscious thinks, 'Excellent, that worked a treat, he didn't
get humiliated by standing up in front of people.' The paradox
is that of course he is still humiliated, by a behaviour designed
to prevent humiliation.

Mr Confident is in the same position. He is looking forward to
giving a speech, and imagines the people laughing at his wit.
When he was young his parents encouraged him by having
him perform stories in front of them to rapturous applause. He
is pretty much in a no-lose situation.

SCENARIO ONE

He stands up and gives his speech, and everyone laughs. Afterwards his unconscious evaluation will be 'That felt good, we must do more.' His conscious evaluation will be, 'Pretty much as I imagined.'

SCENARIO TWO

It is actually a pretty poor speech and gets only scattered laughter. Yet remember the premise, 'what the thinker thinks the prover proves' – because he *thinks* he's good at speeches. Mr Confident's evaluation is likely to be, 'What a miserable bunch!' The only time that this appraisal will change is if the situation is so bad that it takes him over the threshold. This is what happens with a 'loss of confidence'. The event is so powerful that the evaluation causes a shock to the matrix. It needs time and positive reinforcement to get it back fully online again. You see it with football strikers all the time.

In therapy the evaluation phase is very important. After any intervention by the therapist the client must be directed, consciously and while in trance, to notice anything that happens to him or her that is contrary to previous expectation. For example, with Mr Scared, the suggestion would be made that he would notice, and focus all his attention on, times when he feels relaxed in front of people. This reinforces the change in his model of the world begun in the session. Getting him to look for these differences deliberately activates the left brain functions of logic and rational thinking. This will tend to help the client develop a new perspective based on interval and ratio data.

It is like the picture of the young woman/hag you saw earlier. Whichever picture you saw first constitutes the *figure*. All other information in the picture is background (*ground*). You can switch between both versions of the picture, but not hold both at the same time. One is either *figure* or *ground*.

This happens with us all the time. The unconscious filters are constantly deciding for us what information, out of the 2,000,000 bits available, will be *figure* and what will be background. Linking this with the thinker/prover concept means that if you think you lack confidence, the prover will filter information to make sure that only information that proves this to be true will be *figure*, while any information that shows you to be comfortable with people will be deleted (by making it *ground*), or distorted by rationalisation – 'Oh that, that was just luck, it wasn't anything to do with me.'

By directing the evaluation phase to concentrate on the difference, not the sameness, it causes the thinker to focus on information that might once have been *ground*. As it is *'figure'* information that makes up our world, the client's own world begins to look different. Of course, it is not really – it is the client's perception that has shifted. And after all, perceptual shifts are the core business of therapy.

This phase allows for conscious convincing of the unconscious change.

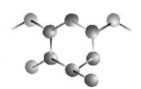

The Matrix Model and creating suggestions

It is always important for therapists to know where they are in the process of treatment, and to know where their client is. The Matrix Model acts as a map to follow, and a means of evaluating change. It also provides part of the answer to step one of Wordweaving™ – identifying what aspect of the client's experience your suggestion is aimed at changing.

Change is possible within each of the parts of the Matrix Model. Indeed, each therapeutic approach from Freud to Cognitive Therapy has tended to focus on one particular area of it. There are techniques that can be employed at each point.

Because this volume is about suggestion, we are going to focus on the need to aim your suggestions at specific points of the model. If you are able to change the client's perception of his or her problem, at any point of the model, then you will change the structure and effect of the problem. Let's begin to see how this is done.

THE FIRST WORDWEAVING™ STEP OF SUGGESTION

Aim each suggestion at a particular point of the Matrix Model or Neuro-logical Level, in order to adapt the client's perception of that point or level.

STIMULUS

This is where most clients try to control the problem – by avoiding the stimulus. Most avoidance will be done unconsciously, but with conscious awareness providing a rationalisation for the action – i.e. 'I'm just not ready for a relationship right now.' What they may actually be doing is avoiding contact with people they could be attracted to (stimulus) because of a fear of rejection or pain etc.

Your suggestion should be aimed at altering the stimulus so that it is perceived as being different in whatever way is appropriate. At this point we can begin to learn how to wordweave. As we look at the factors involved in successful suggestion we will use the problems of three clients as examples. At this stage the suggestions I use as illustrations are not yet as I would deliver them to the client. They are bare frames phrased in a direct form to make the point. You will follow their evolution into something much more elegant and sophisticated (and effective) as the book progresses.

Case 1: Mrs Toothbrush.

Case 2: Mr Bachelor. A thirty-five-year-old man who is successful in his career but has no confidence with women. Whenever he tries to speak to them he blushes and becomes tongue-tied. He has always been insecure in any relationship with women and considers himself unattractive.

Case 3: Mrs Chocolate. A twenty-eight-year-old woman who wants to lose three stone. Has dieted for most of her life but cannot resist chocolate when she is upset or stressed.

Suggestions aimed at changing the perception of the stimulus might include the following:

Mrs Toothbrush: When you see the toothbrush you have a feeling of familiarity. The toothbrush looks and feels comfortable and safe.

Mr Bachelor: When you begin to talk to a woman you notice how she relaxes as you speak easily to her. As you approach the woman you notice feeling relaxed and calm.

Mrs Chocolate: The sight of chocolate reminds you of why losing weight is so important. Chocolate just doesn't look exciting anymore.

MATRIX

The 'engine-room' of the problem is where core change occurs. Any change achieved at any other point within the model will also affect the matrix, indeed that is how the change will have come to work, because it is where the change is stored. This is where regressive techniques focus, and where submodality work has its effect. Suggestion within a regressive technique is likely to be most effective, and, as I explained in a previous sleazy attempt to induce you to buy another book, those specific techniques are going to be my next foray into print.

EMOTION

This has been an area where many hypnotherapists have traditionally focused. They believe that by getting the client to discharge cathartically (cry a lot) – by 'letting the emotion out' – the problem will disappear. The Matrix Model suggests that if that is all the therapist does it will probably reinforce the matrix holding the problem. The emotion can be an effective route into the matrix, but it is re-evaluation of the meaning of the emotion that will cause it to disappear. This is why poor counselling often makes the problem worse. 'How do you feel about that?' is just reactivating and reinforcing the problem.

When aiming suggestions at emotions it mainly involves re-interpreting the feeling as it occurs in the moment, or substituting a new one.

> Mrs Toothbrush: 'There are many things we do that we enjoy the feel of, and when you brush your teeth that feeling of enjoyment can grow stronger each time you do it.' 'That feeling as you pick up the toothbrush can easily be mistaken for anticipation.'

> Mr Bachelor: 'As you feel that feeling as you walk towards a woman you will remember times when you had that feeling just before something worked out really well.' 'It's good to feel a little nervous because it means you are ready to speak to her.'
>
> Mrs Chocolate: 'You notice how proud you feel as you look at chocolate, knowing because of that feeling that you don't want it.' 'The taste of chocolate could actually leave you feeling you shouldn't have bothered.'

RESPONSE

This is the area where behaviourists centre their attention. Extensive focusing on adjusting behaviour can have an effect on the unconscious, eventually, by de-sensitising it. However, it is long, laborious, and has the risk that the unconscious will just replace one poor behaviour with another. NLP techniques such as the 'swish pattern', and various forms of 'anchoring', are appropriate to this part of the matrix. Suggestions aimed at adapting the response could include the following:

> Mrs Toothbrush: 'As you see the toothbrush you run your tongue over your teeth and feel the desire to clean them.' 'And you calmly and deliberately stroke your teeth with the comfortable brush.'
>
> Mr Bachelor: 'As you see the woman approach you to talk you listen to hear what you are about to say.' 'You take a deep breath and relax as you walk up to her.'

> Mrs Chocolate: 'When you see the chocolate you feel yourself shake your head.' 'You firmly say "No I don't want one.".'

 ### TERMINATION

This is an important point to identify in anybody's behaviour. What enabled them to stop? What changed?

> Mrs Toothbrush: 'As you pick up the toothbrush all you notice is the need to clean your teeth.'
>
> Mr Bachelor: 'The blush passes so quickly you hardly notice it at all.'
>
> Mrs Chocolate: 'Any craving you have feels really small.'

 ### EVALUATION

This is a cognitive area, where therapists with that approach tend to focus the client. Again, this can be effective. By getting the client to re-evaluate his behaviour and create new options, it can, over time, re-educate his unconscious and change his matrix. The drawback is that it, too, is hard work for the client, and can take a while. Hypnotic suggestion to focus the client on noticing positive differences can help to re-educate the 'thinker/prover' into recognising that change is occurring more quickly.

Mrs Toothbrush: 'Each time you finish brushing your teeth you recognise how much easier it is.' 'Afterwards you realise you are feeling better about doing it.'

Mr Bachelor: 'Feeling pleased as you walk away because of how much more confident you're becoming.' 'Knowing afterwards that you really enjoyed how different you were feeling as you talked.'

Mrs Chocolate: 'Every time you say no to chocolate means you're getting stronger.' 'Later, looking back, you realise that chocolate is so much less important.'

Building new beliefs and self-identifications by suggestion

To create an effective suggestion you have to know what aspect of a client's reality you want to change, what part of the Matrix Model or Neuro-logical Level you want the client to perceive as different. Within a session you may focus the suggestions on either:

Altering one aspect of the model. This is similar to Erickson's use of splitting, where he sought to take one aspect of a problem and demonstrate to clients their ability to have control over that one aspect, which, by inference, meant they could assume greater control over the whole problem.

or

Cycle through each point in the model, so that within any session your suggestions aim at each part of the problem – the principle being that if you throw enough mud at a wall some is bound to stick.

From what you have read you know the strength of 'I have a problem because I believe I have a problem.' Examine that sentence from a Neuro-logical standpoint and you will recognise that the source of the problem is held at the level of identity, 'I', and belief: 'I believe I have a problem. If I had a belief that it wasn't a problem then that would become true for me, and my prover would prove it.' What this means is that ultimately your suggestions should be aimed at a change in belief and the client's perception of his or her identity. But it is not enough to say repeatedly to the client, 'You are changing what you believe,' or 'Say into the mirror every morning I am confident, I am confident,' which forms the basis of traditional hypnotic ego strengthening. Just saying 'You are a non-smoker' will not be enough in most cases, because there is an unconscious string of experiences that prove the contrary and an evaluation system that maintains the habit.

With Wordweaving™ you link suggestions you make about changes in his or her environment, behaviour or capability (if you are working in Neuro-logical Levels), or stimulus, emotion or response (Matrix Model) to **mean that** (Neuro-logical Level of belief) the problem is changing, as is the client's perception of his or her identity. This linkage can be created by using the algorithms of $C > E$ or $A = B$ (complex equivalence), and created in a number of ways.

Having made suggestions that help them to notice a change in their environment (stimulus or emotion), behaviour (response), or their capabilities, you further suggest the consequence of that is a revised evaluation of their identity or belief. So the suggestions you read of earlier, aimed at changing the clients' perception of their environment, can now be linked to belief or identity in the following ways:

Mrs Toothbrush: 'When you see the toothbrush you notice a feeling of familiarity, **and that means** you can really believe you're changing.' That uses a complex equivalence (A = B), a feeling of familiarity that 'means' she's changing (emotion/environment linked to belief). Such links don't need to be true, they need only to be plausible.

We could use the C > E algorithm by saying '**Because** you feel that feeling of familiarity you recognise you're becoming a different person [*cause* equals feeling of familiarity, *effect* equals change of identity].'

Mr Bachelor: 'When you begin to talk to a woman you notice how she relaxes as you speak easily to her' becomes 'When you begin to talk to a woman you notice how she relaxes as you speak easily to her, and that means you see yourself in a different light,' or 'As you notice how she relaxes as you speak easily to her, you realise you are someone people feel comfortable with.'

Mrs Chocolate: 'The sight of chocolate reminds you of why losing weight is so important' becomes 'Because the sight of chocolate reminds you of why losing weight is so important, you must be changing in yourself' or 'The sight of chocolate reminds you of why losing weight is so important, and that means you can believe you can lose weight.'

When we get to Part III and look at the use of language patterns you will learn that there are several ways of phrasing cause and effect and complex equivalence suggestions, and for many different purposes. For now just practise with the words 'because' (C > E) and 'and that means' (A = B) on the suggestions given earlier on page 61 to link them with belief and identity.

Summary of Part I: Wordweaving™ – the story so far

The first step in Wordweaving™ is to aim the suggestion at a specific level of the client's problem. This involves either a specific point of the Matrix Model, or the Neuro-logical Level that drives it. The purpose of the suggestion is to change the client's perception of that point or level in such a way as to cause a re-evaluation of the problem.

To achieve a change in the client's belief system or self-image it is necessary to provide evidence of why this change might be occurring. One way of doing this is by suggesting a change or difference in his or her perception of the problem environment, behaviour or capability that, when actualised, will have the meaning of change or difference in the belief system or self-image. To achieve this the following ratio is suggested: seventy per cent of suggestions are aimed at environment, behaviour or capability, while thirty per cent are linked to belief or identity. We look at this more closely in Part IV.

To give you practice in identifying the different places to aim, below is a mixture of suggestions and client statements. Identify what part of the Matrix Model or Neuro-logical Level the suggestions are aimed at, or what the client statements originate from.

* 1 Every time I see a bird I freak.
  2 You know cigarettes are not your friend.
  3 Losing weight becomes more and more important to you.
* 4 I feel guilty whenever I say no .
  5 Afterwards you realise it's getting easier.
  6 You notice around you people who enjoy your company.
* 7 I just don't have the will-power.
  8 You are a non-smoker.

9 You breathe easily as you enter the room.

10 I am a loser.

11 Getting on with people just isn't important to me.

12 You notice yourself feeling relaxed and confident.

13 I'm nervous until my boss walks away again.

14 I hear my ex-wife on the phone and I start to sweat.

15 When my part of the meeting is over I'm fine again.

16 You find your determination growing.

17 When it's over I think, never again!

18 You find yourself smiling when it happens.

19 I never get the girl.

20 You talk easily and with authority.

1 Stimulus/environment. 2 Belief. 3 Values. 4 Emotion connected to behaviour (which is a stimulus). 5 Evaluation. 6 Environment. 7 Belief about lack of capability. 8 Identity. 9 Behaviour/response. 10 Identity. 11 Values. 12 Emotion. 13 Termination. 14 Stimulus/environment. 15 Termination. 16. Capabilities. 17 Evaluation. 18 Response. 19 Belief. 20 Behaviour.

The Three Steps of Wordweaving™

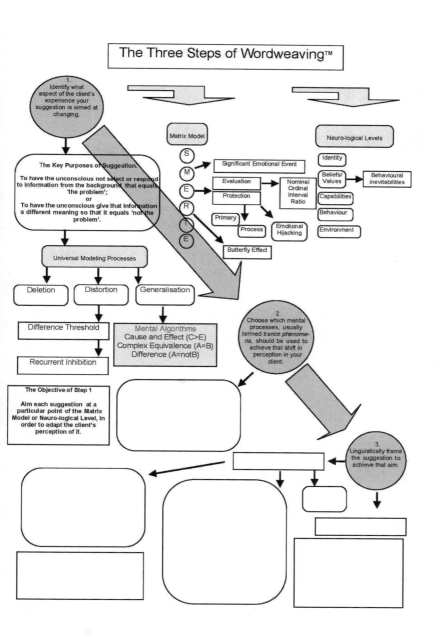

1. Identify what aspect of the client's experience your suggestion is aimed at changing.

The Key Purposes of Suggestion:

To have the unconscious not select or respond to information from the background that equals 'the problem';
or
To have the unconscious give that information a different meaning so that it equals 'not the problem'.

Matrix Model

S
M
E
R
T
E

Significant Emotional Event

Evaluation

Protection

Nominal Ordinal Interval Ratio

Primary

Process

Emotional Hijacking

Butterfly Effect

Neuro-logical Levels

Identity

Beliefs/ Values

Behavioural inevitabilities

Capabilities

Behaviour

Environment

Universal Modeling Processes

Deletion

Distortion

Generalisation

Difference Threshold

Mental Algorithms
Cause and Effect (C>E)
Complex Equivalence (A=B)
Difference (A=notB)

Recurrent Inhibition

2 Choose which mental processes, usually termed *trance phenomena*, should be used to achieve that shift in perception in your client.

The Objective of Step 1

Aim each suggestion at a particular point of the Matrix Model or Neuro-logical Level, in order to adapt the client's perception of it.

3. Linguistically frame the suggestion to achieve that aim.

Part II

Using trance phenomena

Wordweaving™ steps 1 & 2

1 Identify what aspect of the client's experience your suggestion is aimed at changing.

2 Choose which mental processes, usually termed trance phenomena (TP), should be used to achieve that shift of perception in your client.

People most often think of trance as an extraordinary state. In fact it is a naturally occurring experience everybody accesses on a daily basis, and is not some special mental property occurring only as a result of being hypnotised. That said, it has long been thought that hypnotically induced trances are responsible for certain specialised behaviours that are the staple of stage hypnotists – getting their subjects to forget their names, see everybody naked, sleep on command or dance like a chicken. It has been received wisdom that such phenomena can occur only in deeply hypnotised subjects, the so-called 'somnambulists', just as in the older forms of hypnotherapy it was held, and still is in some quarters, that the deeper the trance the more effective any suggestion made would be.

Experiments on trance depth by people such as Hilgard and Weitzenhoffer produced susceptibility scales that based the trance depth of the hypnotised subject on the phenomena that could be demonstrated through them. This added to the belief that certain hypnotic behaviours could be manifested only in a subject who was in a deep state of trance. The Stanford scale suggests that only one in ten people can access this level without special training. Hence the 'deep' part of their description.

These supposedly somnambulistic phenomena include

> Age regression
> Age progression
> Dissociation
> Post-hypnotic suggestion
> Amnesia
> Negative hallucination
> Positive hallucination
> Time distortion
> Sensory distortion

What has come to be recognised by many is that while some behaviours based on TP may require a deep trance state, the TP themselves are something that are experienced by everybody on a daily basis.

As these TP are explained to you, you will see their relationship to the universal modelling processes described earlier. My theory behind Wordweaving™ was given a massive boost by reading the work of Stephen Wolinsky, who had a startling insight into TP. From his work with clients he came to recognise trance states as being the means by which symptoms are created and maintained. Think of every problem as a trance state or series of trance states. Clients arrive with a trance state already present in the symptom, and manifest the trance phenomenon as they describe that problem. This shifts the perspective of hypnotherapy 180 degrees. The job of the therapist becomes that of 'de-hypnotising' the client out of the trance that is being used to hold the symptom together.[24]

Wolinsky is suggesting that the means by which our problem behaviour is actualised is by the manifestation of TP. All problems are trance states as they occur in present time. For example, anxiety is a fear of the future. A client whose presenting problem is anxiety might use a cluster of TPs to synthesise the sensation of anxiety. First comes age progression as she imagines some event in the future going catastrophically wrong, and experiences fear as a result. She hears herself say, 'There is no way I am going to be able to do that' (post-hypnotic suggestion). Negative hallucination (not being able to see something that is there) blocks her ability to see any other options or resources, and possibly time distortion as she feels herself hurtling towards this imagined disaster.

Even what Erickson described as the 'common everyday trance', more popularly described as 'daydreaming', involves a transitory use of TP. Who hasn't heard a song and regressed to a particular memory associated with it; or missed every single word of a conversation because of being engrossed in private thoughts (sensory distortion)? Looked at in this way TP becomes an everyday occurrence, part of what it is to be human, not something extraordinary that occurs only in exceptional circumstances.

According to Wolinsky, all TP involved in the core of the symptom structure of a client's problem have been created by the client as a child in response to a threat. In the Matrix Model this equates to the unconscious developing a protection response to a threatening stimulus. As Wolinsky says,

> 'By the time we reach adulthood we have intricate patterns of defence woven out of clusters of Deep Trance Phenomena that appear to function autonomously within us.'

Choice becomes the key factor in ascertaining whether the trance we are in is part of the problem or part of the solution. For example, I might be in a meeting listening to someone talk. Something she says causes me to stop listening and pay attention to a visual memory. I can choose to bring myself back and focus on her again, or continue my reverie. A problematic trance state occurs if the event produces a response over which we feel we have no control, where there is no range of responses available to us. At that moment we experience having 'no choice' and, as in Figure 5, we plummet

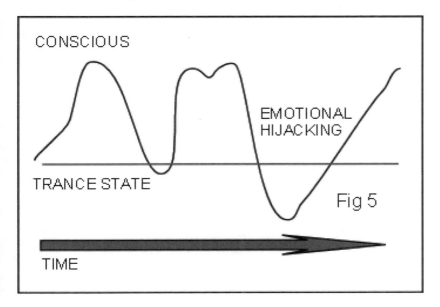

into a trance state through which our response is controlled by the unconscious.

Thinking of trance in this way suggests that consciousness is a continuum, and so are trance states. We meander in and out of each every day. Some states will be pleasant, some not so pleasant. For many clients they will be the stuff of nightmare. Our purpose as therapists is to use suggestion, together with our other techniques, to interrupt, disrupt, or delete the negative trance state, to give the client the choice of being in 'the now'.

In Wolinsky's view there are three core characteristics of trance:

1   A narrowing, shrinking, or fixating of attention;
2   Trance is usually experienced as happening *to* the person;
3   The spontaneous emergence of various hypnotic phenomena.

In a given day a person might experience the 'television trance' where they veg out on the couch for the evening, feeling relaxed and 'tuned out'; their dog might leap onto their lap and demand attention, whereupon they go into a 'doggie trance', talking to it as if they are five years old and becoming totally absorbed playing ball for thirty minutes; the partner gets home and is upset to find no tea has been prepared because of all this play. A 'fight trance' ensues for thirty minutes, before making up and kissing and cuddling on the couch – a 'love trance'.

There are two important aspects to these experiences. The first is that each state has a beginning, middle, and an end. They are processes, and can therefore be manipulated (in the sense of the meaning 'to handle'). The second is that each trance state identified above is comprised of a cluster of TP:

TELEVISION TRANCE

Time distortion – the evening seems to fly by.

Negative hallucination – you are unaware of anything else happening around you.

Sensory distortion – it is only when the dog leaps onto your lap that you realise your neck is cramped and painful.

DOGGIE TRANCE

Age regression – you act in a playful, childlike way, often using baby talk.

Time distortion – playing enjoyably makes the time fly.

FIGHT TRANCE

Age regression – the level of such arguments is usually limited to nominal processing: 'If you cared for me you'd have something cooked!' 'All you want me for is some kind of bloody slave!'

Age progression – at some point either or both might create an image of a never-ending future full of rows and wrongdoings, or the thought 'the rest of the day is ruined.'

Post-hypnotic suggestion – as a result of the age progression they may have the thoughts 'This cannot go on,' or 'I can't bear this much longer.'

LOVE TRANCE

Age regression – the cuddling evokes memories and responses from early childhood, with attendant feelings of comfort, safety, and love.

Time distortion – the evening stands still.

Post-hypnotic suggestion – 'You are the only one for me.'

These clusters are not exhaustive. Each individual, in each situation, could combine trance states into his own unique clusters. It is for the therapist to track and identify them. By doing so it will give you an idea of how to focus your intervention.

You can probably see how the reactions that happen to us in such situations can be described in terms of trance states, where we are literally 'taken over' and are no longer 'ourselves'. The connection between this and what Joseph LeDoux calls 'emotional hijacking' is obvious. These can be short-term behaviours that occur only in a narrow context, such as a spider phobia or public speaking. They can also be more pervasive aspects of the person's personality, something Wolinsky describes as 'hypnotic identity'. This occurs when a set of experiences builds a definition of whom we believe ourselves to be. It might be that that identity is positive, such as 'I am an excellent athlete,' or a negative, 'I am a complete loser.'

Wolinsky's view that TP are 'a means of survival for the overwhelmed child, and the core of the problem structure for the coping adult', fits perfectly within the model of mental functioning we call the Matrix Model.

If we revisit Mrs Toothbrush we can describe what happens in Wolinsky's terms. The stimulus (the toothbrush) causes emotional hijacking, which manifests itself as a TP cluster, perhaps age regression – responding as the eighteen-month-old child did; sensory distortion – attention fixating on the gag reflex; post-hypnotic suggestion – 'If I don't get away I'll be sick,' and perhaps negative hallucination – where all information and resources to deal with the problem differently are hidden from her.

All TP are designed to maintain, support, and protect the integrity of the child. In the early stages of its development the TP are context dependent, but will generalise with a wider range of stimuli (the butterfly effect). They become increasingly distorted, so that a childhood trance response to an authoritarian father could be elicited thirty years later by an altercation with a traffic warden. In this way the structure shifts from an interpersonal trance – from one person to another person, to an intrapersonal trance – from self to self. This intrapersonal trance means that there is nothing in the present situation provoking the reaction other than its trigger – there is no problem outside of the client, everything is happening within the self-to-self trance.

Each child will have a natural preference towards some trance states above others – another reason why the route from stimulus to response varies so greatly in our clients – and will have created them in any situation where their ability to integrate the experience has been exceeded (an SEE). By adulthood we will all have had a lifetime's experience in creating trance responses that have proved most effective at handling particular circumstances.

Unfortunately, because the state was effective in a particular situation it will be generalised with the environment as a whole, meaning that the client experiences the problem 'as it was', and is prevented from being herself in 'present time'. For the duration of the problem clients are truly 'not themselves'.

The use of trance phenomena in treatment

This understanding of trance gives us greater flexibility in helping our clients. If we think of a problem as a non-utilisation of unconscious resources – we are blocked from any way of thinking that could help us – we can see that this is caused by the key characteristic of a trance state; the shrinkage and fixation of attention.

> ## IMPORTANT!
>
> Every suggestion pattern must utilise one or more TP if it is to have any effect.

I think that the most effective suggestions are those that use the same TP that the clients' unconscious use to manifest their problem. If a client creates a problem by a mixture of post-hypnotic suggestion and time distortion, you dissolve that problem using suggestions based on the same two TP.

The major trance phenomena and Wordweaving™

AGE PROGRESSION (PSEUDO-ORIENTATION IN TIME)

We time travel all the time. Whether we are daydreaming about our holiday next week, or a cottage with roses growing round the gate in twenty years' time, age progression can be a pleasant way to spend your time.

Wolinsky believes that age progression is created by

'a series of interpersonal interactions during child-hood that threaten one's psycho-emotional sur-vival, creating a future free of the immediate con-flicts and injuries helps the child get through the day.'

An intrapersonal trance response is thus created over time via repeated use, so that it begins to operate automatically. Conscious intention is no longer required to initiate the trance response. It becomes the means of emotional hijacking.

We have all engaged in flights of fantasy, imagining ourselves as famous, fabulous, or heroic in some way. It is completely normal. When I was sixteen I was going to be the next Barry Sheene. For some, however, who have used it as a primary defence from a grim childhood reality, it becomes an habitual state, where they spend so much time in the fantasy that they lose touch with their actual experience. Clients who have difficulty meeting partners can spend so much time in a fantasy of their life that when they do meet the right person, they never actually date them. The fantasy of the future can be used to resist or deny what is actually happening in the present.

This is a situation where the behaviour moves from context dependence in childhood – the trigger being whatever the child wanted to escape from – to context independence, where it could almost be said that the trigger is now life itself. Such clients drift through life in 'a world of their own', and will be described by people as a Walter Mitty, a dreamer, or a liar.

Age progression is the basis of anxiety. Suppose a client arrives with pre-exam panic. I ask, 'So how do you see it going?' Instantly the client fixes his gaze in a particular direction, and says, 'It'll be a disaster. I'll be nervous, sweating, I'll forget everything, a complete nightmare.' (Notice the post-hypnotic suggestions inherent in his comments, more commonly labelled 'self-fulfilling prophecy'.) Question him more closely and the client can describe the full disastrous picture he has created of this aspect of his future. The unconscious cannot distinguish the difference between an imagined internal representation of an event, and an internal representation of an actual event occurring now in real time, because both are processed using the same brain systems. That is why we can wake from a nightmare with our hearts galloping. Our unconscious will trigger the fight or flight response just as vigorously for an imagined threat as for a real one.

In effect, we are projecting the problem into the future, and the unconscious, in its role of keeping us away from pain, says, 'Well, if that's the future, let's keep away from it.' The client loses motivation, he may even feel depressed. As the event gets closer the unconscious cranks up the anxiety as if it feels that he is somehow not getting the message. By the day of the exam the client is a bag of jelly, and the real event becomes a mirror of the imagined disaster. Once again, paradoxically, the unconscious has created the situation it was seeking to save the client from.

81

The exam phobia is a good example of the most common TP cluster – age regression and age progression. The reason the client creates a negative image of the future is that its matrix match with a past event fits the $A=B$ algorithm (this is the same as that). Once again, the mind does not distinguish between present time information and imagination. Wolinsky estimates that seventy-five per cent of problems have this cluster at the core of symptomology.

Using age progression in suggestions

As you listen to clients describe their problem you will often hear them shift into the consequence of their problem – Mrs Chocolate might say, 'If I keep doing this he'll leave me.' Mr Bachelor might say, 'I don't ever see myself in a happy relationship.' They are both creating a negative future that will probably add fuel to their problem – the thought will upset Mrs Chocolate and probably cause her to seek solace in a Mars Bar, Mr Bachelor may become so depressed by the prospect that he gives up trying to find someone (and so creates the future that depresses him).

Suggestions using this phenomenon are intended to assist the client in imagining a positive future as a consequence of the changes he or she is making now. Using the $C>E$ algorithm, painting a rosy future as the effect of being different now (the cause) creates motivation to continue the change.

Mrs Toothbrush: 'Because you see the toothbrush as the harmless piece of plastic it really is, from today you can look forward to healthy teeth and fresh breath.'

Mr Bachelor: 'Imagine in the future the difference your increasing confidence will make when you see yourself meeting women.'

Mrs Chocolate: 'Every time you say no to chocolate you can see the effect it has on your future.'

Important! Notice how each suggestion has as its focus the assumption of change or difference. The purpose is to sensitise the unconscious to bring to the foreground any information in the background that will confirm, to any degree, that the client's experience of the problem is shifting.

AGE REGRESSION

We all regress, probably every day. When I do something stupid at home I become the 'little boy lost' to my wife in the hope she'll find it cute that I flooded the kitchen. Some hope, but age regression grants me the chance in present-time of using something that worked in the past .

This is only a problem where the adult automatically and unknowingly regresses to get what he wants, where he has no choice or flexibility in his response to a situation. You have probably witnessed people who act like children when angry or upset. Age regression is probably the most commonly experienced TP and is almost always present in any problem. The Matrix Model has explained why this is so.

USING AGE REGRESSION IN SUGGESTIONS

Regressing clients to a point in the past where the problem began in order to change their perception of it is a key element in cognitive hypnotherapy. In the context of this book (the use of suggestion), age regression is limited in its application. Just suggesting that the past can change will not make it so. However, research has shown that people with a tendency to depression tend to remember strings of past experiences that are negative. People with a positive outlook remember positive strings. Using suggestion to get the client to recall past positive experiences and having their unconscious use them as references for future events may improve their outlook. Beyond that keep this use of TP in your pending tray until you have read my next book (another obvious attempt at selling-on, I apologise. Available from all good book stores).

 ## DISSOCIATION

Multiple personality syndrome (MPS) is one of the most amazing conditions known to psychology. The ability of the mind to create complete and distinct personalities, often unknown to each other, becomes all the more bewildering when you read that it is often accompanied by physiological differences as profound as eye colour, shoe size, and even a diabetic/non-diabetic condition.[25]

MPS is usually created by a child in response to severe abuse. It is unlikely that you will have clients present with dissociation to this degree, and unless you are medically or psychiatrically qualified you should refer them via their doctor if you do. However, dissociation is created by many to lesser extents. Dissociation is experienced in three modalities:

1   Dissociation from an internal feeling, sensation, or emotion;
2   Dissociation from a part of the body;
3   Dissociation from external stimuli.

DISSOCIATION FROM AN INTERNAL FEELING, SENSATION, OR EMOTION

Most of us have particular emotions or states that we are unwilling to experience: anger, sadness, fear, guilt, boredom, pain, enthusiasm, and so on. Our attitude towards a particular state is usually established in childhood experiences where parents (or parent figures) invest in that emotion a particular experience. If a child is told 'big boys don't cry,' and approval is dependent on the child's 'not making a fuss', then the adult may keep away from any admission of pain, and block off any conscious experience of it. Hey presto, one emotionally repressed man. If a child is not allowed to express anger, and is sent to her room for every sibling spat, you may end up with an adult who passively accepts any behaviour from others, and never appears wound up. You will have a doormat turn up on your doormat for treatment.

DISSOCIATION FROM A BODY PART

This is actually more common than you might imagine. Sexual dysfunction is a prime example. In the case of impotence the penis may be dissociated from the rest of the body (how many men have names for that part of their body? Wait, I'll ask Percy). I recently saw a female client who had contextual dissociation. She could give herself an orgasm, but could literally feel nothing at all if a man touched her. Another example is a male client who, in one-to-one situations, would lose all feeling in his face, and be unable to put any expression into his speech.

DISSOCIATION FROM EXTERNAL STIMULI:

When the external world is too unpleasant the child learns to 'go inside'. This may be in the form of active conversations with himself, or the creation of a vivid alternative universe. Either way the dissociation removes his psycho-emotional presence from the external environment. Generalised over time you can end up with a person who spends a lot of time inside his head, who feels that he is an observer of life rather than active within it.

Taken at its loosest, all TP are dissociative. Whenever a person is regressing, or progressing, they are dissociated from real time.

USING DISSOCIATION IN SUGGESTIONS

Moving persons into a different perceptual position from the one they occupy while 'doing' their problem can be a very useful tool. It can serve to keep them away from the negative emotion that fuels the problem, and enable them to keep thinking instead of just responding. The three different types of dissociation need to be listened for in order to undo them, and consideration needs to be given to which of the three would be most effectively suggested in the context of any client's problem. For the sake of example I will use a different one for each of our clients. See if you can identify which one I have used with which client (answers at the foot of the page).

1 Mrs Toothbrush: 'As you begin to brush your teeth you will realise that you are not consciously aware of the touch of the brush, it has no feeling where it is in contact with your mouth. You cannot feel it.'

2 Mr Bachelor: 'As you listen to yourself speak to women all you focus on is the words your mouth is forming. You become interested in the words as they emerge, wondering what your mouth will say next.'

3 "Mrs Chocolate: 'You no longer notice the feeling that craves chocolate. That feeling is just forgotten.'

POST-HYPNOTIC SUGGESTION

Traditionally post-hypnotic suggestions are thought of in the stage hypnotist's repertoire as, 'when I click my fingers you will cluck like a chicken.' But they are a powerful tool in a therapeutic context for re-creating a client's

1 Part of the body 2 External stimuli 3 Internal feeling

reality; for example by saying something like 'when you walk into the meeting you will notice how relaxed you feel' (direct suggestion), or 'when you walk into the meeting you might wonder what it will be that makes you realise how relaxed you are' (indirect suggestion). Using post-hypnotic suggestions you can direct a client to any aspect of an experience that his problem would normally have him delete or distort, in order to change his perception of that experience (and his problem). 'And on the morning of the exam you could notice any feeling in your stomach as a sign that you are ready to do well.' Post-hypnotic suggestions are an effective way of influencing the evaluation part of the Matrix Model. By directing the unconscious to notice what you want it to, that will cause a positive evaluation of the behaviour.

As with other TP, post-hypnotic suggestion is created by a series of interpersonal interactions (for example parent-to-child) that are eventually internalised as intrapersonal communications (self-to-self) in the form of what are called introjections – messages received from our environment when we were younger that we continue to accept as the truth without cognitive scrutiny. Transactional analysis suggests that children create a 'lifescript' about themselves, which they then actualise throughout their life. Such a script is supported by a script message – an introjection – such as 'Don't trust men,' 'Life is hard,' 'You are a failure,' or 'Life is great,' 'People are good,' 'You are totally loved' etc. (the latter three don't come to therapy). These are all post-hypnotic suggestions.

If we put these ideas together we have the unsettling insight that a lifescript is a trance state, so most people are living their life in a trance! The task of therapy actually becomes one of waking them up, or de-hypnotising them. In the world of the Matrix it is taking Morpheus's red pill.

Children will tend to respond to introjected post-hypnotic suggestions in one of two ways:

1   Agreement with the suggestion. A child with the message 'I am stupid,' who agrees with it, will shy from competition, advancement, novelty, or challenge.

2   Resist the suggestion. The child who resists the suggestion with a counter-script message, 'I'm not stupid,' may become maniacally competitive, constantly demonstrating her superiority over others, and belittling the achievements of anyone else. No matter how hard the person works, no matter how successful she becomes, she will be driven on because all that is held in the mind is 'I'm stupid.'

 USING POST-HYPNOTIC SUGGESTIONS

The possibilities are endless, but should always include an inherent assumption regarding the unconscious noticing change and difference at some point in the future.

1 Mrs Toothbrush: 'As you walk into the bathroom and see the toothbrush you will notice how you feel relaxed.'

2 Mr Bachelor: 'When you see the next woman you are attracted to you become aware of that feeling of relaxation as you begin to talk to her.'

3 Mrs Chocolate: 'Last thing at night you will look back and realise how you have forgotten about chocolate all day [includes use of amnesia].'

AMNESIA

Amnesia is one aspect of hypnosis that the general public are likely to be aware of. It is one of the major concerns they generally arrive with at my office – that they will be 'out' and not be aware of what I am doing. I have never considered any therapeutic advantage it might give to be worth the possible risk of false allegations. It may naturally occur; it is perfectly normal for a client to report that they were not aware of everything I said – that is amnesia, and is very useful. But they do not report that they were unaware of everything that was occurring, and they still feel in control.

Amnesia has been present in therapy since the beginning. Freud's concept of the unconscious repressing material can be classified as amnesia. So can the more modern term 'denial'. The everyday experience of 'forgetting' is another example. Amnesia goes on all the time, from losing the car keys, to forgetting dinner with the in-laws, to being stomach-pumped at the age of eighteen months.

As a trance state it is created to protect the child from an experience that cannot be adequately processed. It is common when first initiating the client into a session of regression for their mind to go blank. Actually developing that 'blank state' by exploring the sub-modality qualities of the blankness can often release the client from the trance state and the repressed memory suddenly appears. Wolinsky would probably say that by doing so we are working with the client's own trance state, and then de-hypnotising them from it.

The opposite of amnesia is also a problem's common component. Hypermnesia is the remembering of everything. In the context of a problem the client will be able to describe in exquisite, agonising detail, every facet of the experience. Is that more or less likely to make the problem worse? In that situation the suggestion of amnesia can be a useful antidote – 'It is normal to *forget*. We *forget* all the time. I wonder what it is about this experience that your unconscious would find easiest to forget first – because it can be easy just to *forget*....

The next thing it forgets could be something similar or different... and at some point we could wonder what the unconscious might choose to forget that would help you the most to *let go of the effects of this memory* [italicised words semantically marked to make them commands].' The above is a taster of the use of language patterns we develop later.

In everyday life a person who developed this state in childhood will continue to use it in adulthood – and very useful it can prove, after all, for who doesn't want a good memory? For the child who used it as a defence, by remembering everything the parent said to prevent him being punished, he will often develop into a mistrustful adult who can remember five years later every word of an argument, promise or insult.

USING AMNESIA IN SUGGESTIONS

If I say to you don't think of a blue tree, what comes to your mind? That's right, a blue tree. The mind cannot process a negative, so you have to think of the thing you are trying not to think about. This is the structure of obsession and craving. The more your clients say to themselves I mustn't have a cigarette, the more they are forcing themselves to think of having one. A general rule in hypnotic language is to say things in the way you want the client to think of them, to make your language positive. In most cases it is a good rule. If you go back over our three clients you will see that I have broken this rule several times. See if you can identify where. There are specific ways to use negative suggestions that are appropriate and effective. For example:

1 Mrs Toothbrush: 'Try to not notice how safe the toothbrush looks as you pick it up.'

2 Mr Bachelor: 'I don't want you to notice too often how much more confident you are feeling.'

3 Mrs Chocolate: 'Don't let your tongue think of X (her worst food) whenever you taste chocolate.'

In the use of amnesia you can suggest that they forget the thing you want them to forget, but this has the danger of bringing it back to mind – as in 'Forget to be anxious.' I prefer to cause them to forget by guiding their awareness into something else. This is a use of hypermnesia. By filling their seven plus-or-minus two bits of conscious awareness with any information other than the thing you want forgotten, you relegate it to the ninth or tenth thing available to awareness, and is the same as forgetting.

1 Mrs Toothbrush: 'All the time you are brushing your teeth your mind is busy reviewing all the things you've done during the day. All the time the brush is moving up and down or side to side you are focused on remembering everything about your day.'

2 Mr Bachelor: 'It's only when you walk away from the girl that you realise you forgot to remember to be nervous.'

> 3 Mrs Chocolate: 'With chocolate there are so many other things to think about, good, positive things that fill your mind, all the way through the day remembering to think about everything that helps you forget about it.' In this example I have mentioned the thing to be forgotten, but I have split the word chocolate from forgetting by placing them at opposite ends of the sentence and implying it by the word 'it'. That tends to reduce the blue-tree effect.

NEGATIVE HALLUCINATION

We have all experienced searching for keys, and having them turn up under our noses when we look a second time; or the realisation that someone is looking at us expectantly for an answer when we haven't heard a word they've said; or suddenly finding our leg is painfully cramped after being absorbed in an interesting programme. Each of the above is a negative hallucination, the first visual, the second auditory, and the third kinaesthetic. The word 'negative' does not denote a value, only that the phenomenon deletes an aspect of our potential experience – something we *could* notice, but don't. You may know someone whose partner is having an affair, and it must be obvious to her because it is to everybody else, yet somehow she remains oblivious.

In NLP terms we would refer to the process of *deletion* or *distortion* that makes this possible. Wolinsky would claim this as TP in action. The information is too painful to contemplate so the person creates a trance state to keep it at bay. How often do people in this situation seem to be 'in a world of their own'?

As with the other TP, negative hallucination is more common than is generally recognised. My parents separated when I was twenty-two and I was profoundly shocked at suddenly being confronted by these two, weak, fallible, sometimes childish, people. *These* weren't *my* parents. But of course they were – they simply weren't the iconic stereotypes I had constructed during a childhood that perceived them as strong and omnipotent. As with most children (given half a chance), I had deleted or distorted aspects of their behaviour, which made me feel less safe – their weakness, their fallibilities, their frailties. The need to recognise our parents' own humanity is a developmental stage that many people never pass through successfully.

This particular TP example contains elements of all the others. One is contact with our parents. It can send us into a trance state where we behave differently, we feel differently, and where we persist in seeing them 'as they have always been'. The effect of ageing in our parents is a thing that most struggle with, and the unconscious of many will negatively hallucinate whatever makes us more comfortable. It will also be true of many aspects of other relationships. The saying 'love is blind' is a prime example, and when the first glow begins to fade the lover begins to perceive the partner differently. 'He's changed,' is the cry. No, he hasn't: her friends could always see he was an inconsiderate pig. She has negatively hallucinated that behaviour out of her awareness. TP can be seen as the mechanism by which attention is fixated on particular information (figure), and kept away from other data (ground).

*U*SING NEGATIVE HALLUCINATION IN SUGGESTIONS

Negative hallucination is part of all trance experiences, because if trance is achieved by fixation on a small area of experience, then that presupposes the mind is not aware of everything that is not that small area. In a therapeutic trance the client can be guided to stop noticing the negative, to redirect attention to 'not noticing' something else and by focusing on a positive. The examples I gave for amnesia demonstrate negative hallucination. By not noticing something (negative hallucination) the client develops amnesia towards it. Similarly time distortion is useful to create negative hallucination, as in 'It's not until afterwards that you realise you didn't even notice.' This avoids the same problem that can occur with amnesia, of not bringing directly to mind the very thing you don't want them to notice.

POSITIVE HALLUCINATION

This condition is the flip side of hallucination – the seeing, hearing, or feeling of things that are not physically present. This is most commonly associated with people suffering from psychosis or high on drugs. However, as with the other TP, it begins in childhood. It is common for children to have an imaginary friend, to be afraid of what is in the dark, to experience the most extraordinary adventures in their play. For years I gave my brother ten suggestions for 'dreams' every night – adventures he could fall asleep to, all of them potential hallucinations.

Looked at in this way our imagination is a trance state, every daydream, every fantasy, involves us experiencing what does not exist, and responding to it physiologically. As hypnotherapists it will be commonplace to have clients experience lying on their favourite beach while in trance, and reporting later that they could feel the sun on their face.

Clients will also often report how they feel 'excluded', how they know people don't like them by the look they can see on their faces, how their partners makes them feel stupid and worthless just by the tone of their voice. All of these can be examples of this phenomenon. It can be a pervasive presence in their everyday life. Karen Horney, the famous psychoanalyst, identified three types of people: those who move towards others; those who move away from others; and those who move against others. With the latter type you find that they feel constantly in the presence of opposition. For them 'life is a battle.' They can be very prickly, take offence easily, and pick a fight with a mirror. These people positively hallucinate the reactions of others as being oppositional, distorting their responses to fit what their beliefs dictate.[26]

All people who report anxiety will have such TP as part of their cluster, because they are responding to something that is not present, not currently happening, or is not known. They are manifesting an object, person or situation and placing it in their future (age progression). Therapy involves getting them to hallucinate something better. After all, if all future is fabrication, we might as well fabricate something nice!

USING POSITIVE HALLUCINATIONS IN SUGGESTIONS

Distorting the information coming in through the senses of your clients so that it is interpreted positively is a vital part of most sessions. After all, they have come to see you to help them see life differently. We have already looked at age progression, which can be thought of as an internal, positive hallucination (i.e. in the imagination). This time we are going to make the hallucination external, so that they perceive something outside of themselves in a different way.

Mrs Toothbrush: 'When you see the toothbrush you notice all the things about it that make it useful and safe.'

Mr Bachelor: 'As you converse with women you notice how relaxed they feel in your company and the way they look that lets you know they're enjoying the conversation.'

Mrs Chocolate: 'In the supermarket you feel yourself finding the look of fruit more and more appealing.'

TIME DISTORTION

A famous quantum physicist once said that we invented time so that things didn't happen all at once. In the realm of the quantum the possibility exists that everything that has happened, is happening, and that could ever happen, is happening, every moment, all the time.

I hope you didn't read that first thing on a Monday morning, because it is a big thought to start the week with. I introduce it only to have you think about the nature of time. 'Clock time' is our objective experience – Macbeth's 'time that moves through the roughest day'. Shakespeare needed to remind us of this because we all have days that seem never-ending; conversely we also have days that fly. This is the subjective nature of time, and Wolinsky argues that our distortion of its passage is a trance state, learnt in childhood to make happy times last longer, and bad times pass quickly.

Once again we find the unconscious paradox: the more the passage of time is resisted, the slower it passes. It may be a by-product of the fight or flight response, where danger causes our focus to become so narrow that the event seems to occur in slow motion. Perhaps the action of endorphins, released in response to pleasure, has the opposite effect.

The subjective quality of time means that it can be distorted in a number of ways. A person who believes that she is stupid may achieve ten good things in a day, but looking back will recall only the one mistake she made. The bad event is 'stretched' to make it a 'bad day', and the good events are compressed to the point where they can be forgotten (amnesia).

The same will be true of relationship issues. A couple coming to see you will not be remembering the successful and happy ten years they have had together. If questioned they will fly through that period in seconds. Their focus will be on the last three months, and each will be able to catalogue in minute detail the shortcomings of the other during that period.

USING TIME DISTORTION IN SUGGESTIONS

There are many uses for time distortion. You can make negative moments pass more quickly, just as you can make positive events last longer or appear more often. I have found this to be one of the most useful TP of all, because if you can get the client to perceive the problem as happening less often, or lasting less time, it suggests to him that the problem is changeable. After that we are just negotiating about how changeable. An example is a client I had with obsessive compulsive disorder. She had to check everything sixteen times – the light switches, the front door, everything. Initially I worked on reducing the number of times. This worked well, her compulsion reduced to four times for a while, but then gradually returned. I tried something else. Instead of adjusting the number of times I played with time itself. I introduced her to the idea of the unconscious being able to process 2,000,000 bits of information per second, while we can consciously work only much slower. In trance I suggested that in the time it took her to check something twice consciously, her unconscious can have checked it sixteen times. So her unconscious can continue to have the compulsion – just so quickly that she is no longer aware of it.

Mrs Toothbrush: 'Even though you brush your teeth thoroughly it will feel like it is over in seconds.'

Mr Bachelor: 'You enjoy talking to women so much that your time with them seems to fly.'

Mrs Chocolate: 'It is only when it is time for your next meal that you realise how quickly the time has gone since the last.'

SENSORY DISTORTION

Sensory distortion is where bodily experiences are either amplified or dulled. In the case of dulling there is an obvious crossover with dissociation. An extreme case of distortion is phantom limb pain, where the patient continues to feel pain from an amputated limb.

Other examples include:

Anorexia, where the client focuses attention on the stomach, and feels bloated or fat following the smallest mouthful of food. She can also distort the taste of food into something horrible, and numb the feeling of hunger.

Premature ejaculation often occurs because of an over-sensitisation of the tip of the penis.

Panic attacks often occur because the unconscious becomes overly sensitive to normal bodily occurrences, such as a sudden change in heart rate, or blushing.

There are three different types of sensory distortion:

1 Psychophysiological sensory distortion, in which unwanted sensations are numbed, dulled, or overly intensified. The anorexia numbing hunger is a prime example. When I used to run cross-country as a boy (and hated it) my mind would say 'How am I doing, do I have a stitch yet?' My attention would create it, and my continued focus on it would magnify it until I had to stop running.

2   Hyper- or hypo-sensory distortion, in which environmental stimuli are amplified or obliterated. Tinnitus can be an example of this (where it is not caused by physiological damage). Another is where a normal pressure is applied to a particular part of the body but is experienced as being acutely painful. This is often caused by a trauma. I had a client who was attacked when she was a child and pulled by her left forearm into a bush. The pain and fear of that experience became linked with the pressure on her arm that could be triggered by anybody duplicating the pressure (an anchor).

3   Pain sensory distortion, in which only the afflicted portion of the body is affected.

USING SENSORY DISTORTION IN SUGGESTIONS

Our senses can be easily fooled. It is easy to confuse a hot object with a cold object under certain conditions, just as it is easy initially to mistake a taste you hate for a taste you like, simply because you expected it to be so. Sensory distortion can be used to alter the taste of a cigarette into something awful. It can be used to change the perception of a feeling, such as nervousness, into something more useful – like anticipation. As mentioned earlier someone enjoying a roller coaster probably labelled the feeling in their stomach as excitement. If they heard the bolt snap under their seat that feeling would probably transform to blind fear. Yet if blood were taken from them just before and just after the bolt snapped, the chemicals that equal fear and excitement would be the same. It is our interpretation of that sense that makes it good or bad. This means that all sensory data is available to distortion, and visual hallucination is one form of sensory distortion. The way it tends to be thought of in this context is the distortion of kinaesthetic, auditory or gustatory (taste) information.

Mrs Toothbrush: 'As the soft bristles of the brush gently brush your teeth and gums you notice how comforting it feels.'

Mr Bachelor: 'You become used to that feeling in your stomach as you meet women to mean that you are excited by the prospect of enjoying their company.'

Mrs Chocolate: 'And you notice how the taste of chocolate changes as the days go by, enjoying it less and less.'

Summary of Part Two: Wordweaving ™ – the use of trance phenomena within suggestions

Hypnotherapy is about the utilisation of trance states, both those that you induce in the client, and those that the client brings into the room with him. Traditionally only the former have been recognised. By being aware of both you become much more flexible and powerful in the help you can give.

Every problem a client brings you can be seen as consisting of either a single or a cluster of the TP mentioned above. Sometimes it will be useful to think of them in this way, and view your intervention as being de-hypnotic.

Clients will present with a negative consequence of these phenomena. Our suggestions utilise the fact that every trance phenomenon also holds the possibility of alleviating the problem by reversing its effect. For example:

> Sensory distortion can be used to turn a pleasure, like chocolate, into something unpleasant. It can also be used to turn an unpleasant feeling, like anxiety, into something neutral or positive, like anticipation or excitement.

Negative hallucination can get the client to fail to notice what he would usually notice that triggers his problem. If sweaty palms alert him to feelings of anxiety you can make suggestions that divert his attention away from his palms. He may cease to notice spiders, or become oblivious to those stimuli that used to make him feel inadequate.

Positive hallucination is all about distorting external reality into something positive. It can be used to make a client's audience appear happy and interested in what she is saying; to notice those things around her that mean she is changing.

Time distortion can be used to make an interview fly by, to make panic attacks end sooner, or for positive events to last longer.

Dissociation: to reduce pain; to increase control of an emotion by observing the trigger from the third-person point of view; or to reduce anxiety.

Amnesia: to forget anything that is negative, or anything that is a trigger for a problem.

Post-hypnotic suggestion can direct attention to something in the future that will sensitise the unconscious to change or difference. It can suggest a known quantity that the client will encounter as having a useful significance.

Age progression: to discover resources in the future that can be utilised now, and to build a positive outcome.

And of course,

Age regression can be used to access resources from the past and bring them forward to the present. Obviously it can also be used for regression, to de-potentiate an SEE. The list is extensive, and limited only by your own creativity.

Read the following examples and identify the TP involved. Answers overleaf:

1 It's only afterwards, looking back, that you realise how confident you felt.
2 Whenever I think of it I see myself old and lonely.
3 And you just forget to think about whether the pain is there or not.
4 I feel hungry all the time.
5 Later you notice you are feeling more comfortable.
6 You just don't notice the audience.
7 Everyone looks at me funny.
8 He makes me feel like I'm a kid.
9 I just spend my life watching myself screwing up.
10 When my boss asks me a question it's like time stands still and I'm trapped.
11 Opening up before you is a future full of possibility.
12 I've forgotten what it felt like to be happy.

13 As you enter the room that feeling in your stomach becomes a feeling of anticipation.

14 On the way home I think, 'I'm bound to get angry about this.'

15 I just can't see that he cares.

16 You see the spider looking weak and scared.

17 You find yourself remembering how easy it felt when you were younger .

18 It can be fun to watch yourself as you make the shot look easy.

EXERCISE

In each of the following identify what TP are being used to create the client's problem, and write down what uses of particular TP could be used to alter their perception usefully.

Mr Nibble chews his nails whenever he starts to feel anxious. He feels that it comforts him and distracts him away from the nervous feeling in his stomach. It seems to slow him down.

Ms Jumpy is terrified of travelling in lifts. She is scared of getting trapped if one breaks down, she feels as if there isn't enough air and that she'll suffocate if it gets stuck. 'Nobody will rescue us in time.'

---

1 Time distortion. 2 Age progression. 3 Amnesia. 4 Sensory distortion. 5 Post-hypnotic suggestion. 6 Negative hallucination. 7 Positive hallucination. 8 Age regression. 9 Dissociation. 10 Time distortion. 11 Age progression. 12 Amnesia. 13 Sensory distortion. 14 Post-hypnotic suggestion. 15 Negative hallucination. 16 Positive hallucination. 17 Age regression. 18 Dissociation.

Mr Anxious is experiencing panic attacks. Whenever he feels his heart race, or his face flush, he thinks 'Oh my God, a heart attack, I'm going to die!' and he gets breathless and has a panic attack. His father died young from this condition.

Now that we have covered steps one and two we can now look at the third Wordweaving™ step – how to frame the suggestion linguistically.

ANSWERS

Mr Nibble – sensory distortion; time distortion.

Ms Jumpy – sensory distortion; age progression/post-hypnotic suggestion.

Mr Anxious – age progression; age regression (to father's death).

The Three Steps of Wordweaving™

1. Identify what aspect of the client's experience your suggestion is aimed at changing.

The Key Purposes of Suggestion.

To have the unconscious not select or respond to information from the background that equals 'the problem';

or

To have the unconscious give that information a different meaning so that it equals 'not the problem'.

Matrix Model

S
M
E
R
T
E

- Significant Emotional Event
- Evaluation
- Protection
- Primary
- Process
- Emotional Hijacking
- Nominal Ordinal Interval Ratio
- Butterfly Effect

Neuro-logical Levels

- Identity
- Beliefs/ Values → Behavioural inevitabilities
- Capabilities
- Behaviour
- Environment

Universal Modeling Processes

- Deletion
- Distortion
- Generalisation

- Difference Threshold
- Recurrent Inhibition

Mental Algorithms
Cause and Effect (C>E)
Complex Equivalence (A=B)
Difference (A=notB)

2. Choose which mental processes, usually termed *trance phenomena*, should be used to achieve that shift in perception in your client.

The Objective of Step 1

Aim each suggestion at a particular point of the Matrix Model or Neuro-logical Level, in order to adapt the client's perception of it.

Positive Hallucination
Negative Hallucination
Age Progression
Age Regression
Sensory Distortion
Time Distortion
Amnesia
Dissociation
Post Hypnotic Suggestion

3. Linguistically frame the suggestion to achieve that aim.

Important!

Every suggestion pattern must utilise one or more trance phenomena if it is to have any effect.

Part III

Linguistic framing

The three steps of Wordweaving ™

1 Identify what aspect of the client's experience your suggestion is aimed at changing.
2 Choose which mental processes, usually termed 'trance phenomena', should be used to achieve that shift in perception in your client.
3 **Linguistically frame the suggestion to achieve that aim.**

There are two main ways that you can frame suggestions: you can either use direct suggestion, or indirect suggestion. Over the years these two approaches have become dichotomous camps – therapists tend to classify themselves as either direct or permissive. It is one of those situations where a choice is made when no choice is necessary and has resulted in a sterile argument over which is better. Research has consistently shown that both methods work equally well. My point of view is that if both methods of framing can be effective, but neither is effective with all people all the time, then this would suggest that we should match the method to the client, and become more aware of what other factors are involved in whether the suggestion is accepted by the recipient – in whatever style it is delivered.

When I first learnt hypnosis I was taught only direct suggestion, and I became so disillusioned with the random nature of its success that I never really returned to it. Even after I learned the indirect approach I depended more on regression and NLP techniques and tried to avoid relying solely on suggestion. In fact in my early years, if I conducted a session with a client that did rely solely on suggestion I felt as if I was cheating, because I wasn't convinced that results from suggestion were anything more than placebo.

And yet clients would often return after such a session and report improvements that mirrored the suggestions I had made. For a while I continued to write it off as placebo or the suggestibility of the client, but it happened often enough to trigger my curiosity and wonder 'could something else be going on that made a suggestion work beyond simply whether it was delivered directly or indirectly?'

That began the re-evaluation that transformed my opinion about the power of suggestion, and has led to this book. I admit to a bias in favour of indirect suggestion, so please be aware of that as you read on. However, the bias is much less pronounced than it used to be, largely because of my friendship with Gil Boyne. Gil is a master hypnotherapist who ranks beside Milton Erickson as one of the giants in the field. He is also unashamedly direct in his approach – with forty years of great results to show for it. Without his influence this book would have been much more arrogantly certain of the superiority of indirect suggestion, and would have missed the point that lies at the heart of Wordweaving™ – that it is matching the words you weave to the uniqueness of each client's private world, which is the most important factor.

What I continue to believe is that suggestions that cause clients to use their own model of the world to gain the outcome you desire, and which involve the minimum contamination from the therapist's own model of the world, are most likely to be effective in most cases. For that reason I tend to use indirect language forms most of the time, becoming more direct as the therapeutic relationship develops and improves.

Other factors that will cause me to be more direct are where I find the client is highly suggestible, or where I think that the client's personality is more suited to a direct approach (one example of this is the client who brings a list of what he thinks he needs to hear to get better), some people from a service background, or people born before 1950 are other likely candidates (my apologies to those who are offended by those generalisations: I obviously didn't mean you, and I did only say 'likely'!).

Direct suggestion

To clarify the terms more precisely, direct suggestion is where the therapist tells the client what it is that he is experiencing, or what it is that he will or will not experience in the future. The examples used to illustrate the use of trance phenomena mainly used direct suggestion for the sake of simplicity, not because they are necessarily most effective, e.g.

Mrs Toothbrush: 'When you see the toothbrush you notice all the things about it that make it useful and safe.'

Mr Bachelor: 'As you converse with women you notice how relaxed they feel in your company and the way they look that lets you know they're enjoying the conversation.'

Mrs Chocolate: 'In the supermarket you feel yourself finding the look of fruit more and more appealing.'

In each of the above the client is told how he or she is going to respond. This can be very effective in the right circumstances and with the right client. If the suggestion is appropriate and is accepted by the client then it will work. If it does not fit the client's model of the world, or the client resists the idea for whatever reason, then it will be ineffectual. An example is where in my early days I was taught to relax people by describing a beach they could walk along. One day a female client burst into tears as I attempted this induction, because she had broken up with her boyfriend that summer – on a beach. They are not relaxing places to all people.

Indirect suggestion

The use of indirect language has largely been popularised by the work of Milton Erickson.

Before Erickson, the commonly held view (which is still not extinct) was that it was the power of the trance alone that rendered the hypnotist's words influential, not the words themselves. We now know this is not true. In his early days Erickson performed an experiment on an unknowing secretary who suffered from migraines. During such attacks he got her to take his dictation of meaningless gobbledygook from psychotic patients, but within which he had layered suggestions aimed at mediating the migraine. The migraines disappeared in under ten minutes. As a control to the experiment, on other such occasions he gave dictation with the suggestions removed, and her migraine remained.

Clearly she was not in what was traditionally recognised as a trance state, but the words themselves had an effect.

The way that Erickson used language was the result of incredible dedication to his craft, not just his undeniable genius. He spent many hours analysing the effects of particular phrasing, methods of delivery, and the moulding of suggestion to each client. We benefit from his fascination and dedication of over more than seventy years. As with Gil

Boyne and Dave Elman, we truly are standing on the shoulders of giants.

When Bandler and Grinder studied his work from an NLP point of view – to discover the 'how' of how he got the results he got – they coined the term 'artful vagueness' to describe his approach. This has been misinterpreted by many who describe themselves as 'Ericksonian'. It does not mean being vague about what you want the client to do, to weave dense metaphors around the issue, or to speak in a low gravelly monotone while fixing the client in the beam of your hypnotic gaze.

Erickson believed that we all have the resources within ourselves to find a solution to a problem. He once said the reason clients come is that they are out of contact with their unconscious minds. For him the process of therapy is the reintroduction of the client to his strengths, abilities and qualities that the problem causes him to ignore. As therapists we are guides in that journey, not gods giving them something they previously lacked.

With that view, Erickson was very precise in what he wanted his clients to achieve, the objective he was pursuing, but he trusted they could find their own way to it. That is where the artful vagueness of his language came into play. His suggestions left his clients needing to make their own sense of them. They had to fill in the blanks. He talked of what his clients could or might experience, not what they had to. For example, instead of saying, 'As you relax you will feel your arms getting heavier,' he might say, 'You might wonder what you would feel that would let you know you are relaxing.' This indirect form of suggestion tends to overcome resistance to the suggestion, because the client is not being told what to do. It lets the client use his own model of the world to fulfil Erickson's objective. So, instead of imposing my beach on a client I will say something like, 'If there was a place, the safest and most relaxing place you could go now, what it would be around you in that place that reminds you of why it is so relaxing? The things you can see, hear in that place, feel, that allow you to sink

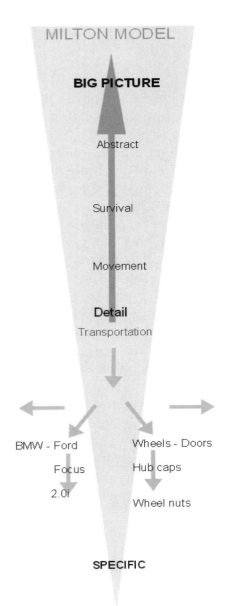

Fig 6
Hierarchy of Ideas

MILTON MODEL

BIG PICTURE

Abstract

Survival

Movement

Detail

Transportation

BMW - Ford   Wheels - Doors

Focus   Hub caps

2.0i   Wheel nuts

SPECIFIC

deeper and deeper into the memory.'

I need have no idea of where my clients actually go, and do not contaminate them with my ideas of what is relaxing. They themselves are able to build the image in the best possible way, and they are doing what I want, yet after their own fashion.

In a nutshell, the art of indirect suggestion is to be clear in your own mind about what you want your clients to achieve, but to leave them the maximum flexibility in how they themselves achieve it. An inherent belief within the system is that self-generated change is more powerful and long-lasting than any change that's perceived as imposed, forced, or suggested from the outside.

Bandler and Grinder developed a model of indirect language from their study of Erickson's work. They called it the Milton model.

To begin to understand the Milton model we need to turn to the concept of surface and deep structure that derived from the *Transformational Linguistics* of Chomsky (drop that phrase into an NLP dinner party if you want to make a cheap impression!).[27]

The hierarchy of ideas

If you look at the diagram on the previous page we'll begin with the word 'transportation', though we could begin anywhere.

From this point a conversation could go in one of three directions: We could 'chunk' down to look for more detail, by asking questions from the NLP meta-model. Or, 'What are examples of this?' The reply might be 'Cars'.

We could explore laterally from the point of 'cars' by 'chunking' up to transportation again, and asking, 'What are other examples of transportation?' This is how you 'do' lateral thinking, moving up one level of abstraction, and then 'chunking' across. The answer might this time be 'Planes'.

Finally we could look for the bigger picture by 'chunking' up to a higher level of abstraction, asking 'For what purpose is transportation?' or 'What is the intention of....?' For this particular person the answer might be 'Movement'. (What would be the answer for you?)

Each has a different purpose within the therapeutic relationship: 'chunking down' can recover deletions, distortions and generalisations from the client and acquaint her with the deep structure meanings that influence her problem; 'chunking across' can assist with reframing her problem; and 'chunking up' can bring to light the unconscious intention behind the problem – its purpose.

Taking a client in the same direction for any length of time will involve her in a trans-derivational search (TDS), where she is seeking deep-structure meanings. This is trance-inducing, because it is causing her to fixate to a deeper and deeper degree on her internal processes. This is one of the reasons why your clients can be in trance and open to your suggestions long before you begin a formal induction.

The basis of the Milton model is that by the specific use of vague and ambiguous language you cause your clients to search for the meaning of what you are saying from within their deep structure, and discover the resources within to solve their problem. The simplest example I can think of is one you are already familiar with. Instead of 'Lie on a beach and relax,' you suggest "If you were to go to the most relaxing place you've ever been, where would it be?' The resultant TDS brings from the clients' deep structure the most appropriate resource for them to do what you want them to do.

The work of Bandler and Grinder has categorised many of the patterns of speech present in Erickson's work. Appropriate use of these patterns can have a profound effect on your client, but what is sometimes forgotten is the pains Erickson went to with each client. His true genius was to weave his sublime use of language seamlessly into the client's model of the world. So please remember, the Milton model is a key skill to master, but it does not stand alone. Aimless use of the Milton model is just waffle. One of my purposes in creating the Wordweaving™ system was to help therapists make the Milton model useable – to make their vagueness artful.

Within the context of hypnotherapy I have found one part of the Milton model to be particularly important when making suggestions – what are known as 'presuppositions'. They serve as a useful introduction to the model as a whole.

Presuppositions

"What is the question that I can ask which by the very nature of the of the presuppositions in the question itself will cause the client to make the greatest amount of change by having to accept the presuppositions inherent in the question?"

Tad James, 1992[28]

Presuppositions are the linguistic equivalents of assumptions, and are present in most sentences. If I say that I am writing this in the office in my house there is an assumption that it is not the only room in the house, but it is not explicitly stated, and most people will not even be aware that their mind has made this assumption to make sense of the sentence. That is the power of presuppositions. Their use can cause the clients' unconscious to accept something without even knowing that they have accepted it, thereby bypassing resistance.

POSSIBILITY

If I say to a client, 'You will feel more relaxed,' this is an order that the client may resist. If I say, 'You may find yourself feeling more relaxed,' it introduces the idea of feeling more relaxed as a possibility, which is less likely to be rejected. Words like 'may', 'might' and 'could' are all presuppositions of possibility. Instead of 'You will notice feeling more confident,' the suggestion can be framed as, 'You may notice feeling more confident,' 'You could notice feeling more confident.'

CAUSE AND EFFECT (C > E)

You have already met this as an algorithm of the brain, which is one reason why this is such an important language pattern. Cause and effect as a presupposition works by linking one thing happening, to something else happening. It does not need to be true, it needs only to be plausible. If I say, 'You will learn new things while you relax,' that may be resisted. If I say, 'Because you're relaxing your mind is open to new ideas,' the idea is plausible, not necessarily true, but the strange power of the word 'because' comes into play and makes it more acceptable. In an experiment a person entered a copy room in an office where there was a queue of people waiting to photocopy. She said, 'Can I go to the front, please?' Whenever this was done the result was the same –

overwhelmingly people objected. If, however, she said, 'Can I go to the front because I have only one copy to take?' sixty per cent of the time she was allowed to, even though some of those waiting also had only one copy. Since Newton we expect to live in a cause-and-effect universe, so we seem adapted to respond to things when given a reason for them (i.e. a cause). There are several ways of forming C>E statements other than the use of 'because'. The structure 'if X then Y', or 'as you X then you Y' achieves it, as does the use of the verb 'to make':

'If you allow yourself to relax then you sink deeper.'

'As you notice your confidence growing then you become aware of feeling differently around people.'

'That feeling of peace makes you realise how you are changing.'

COMPLEX EQUIVALENCE (A = B)

Another of those brain algorithms, so again very important. This is where the mind takes two separate things and treats them as meaning the same. It is similar in style to a C>E statement, except that in the way it is phrased a complex equivalence has two things existing simultaneously as in A=B, or 'A means the same as B', whereas a C>E has the effect happening after the cause, so time is a consideration – first one thing then the next.

'The learning your unconscious takes from this session means you can notice many changes.'

'You're sitting in this chair and that means you can relax.'

AWARENESS

The presupposition of awareness uses the fact that the things we pay conscious attention to moment to moment are selected by the unconscious. Suggestions using this presupposition are aimed at guiding the unconscious of the client to notice, i.e. be aware of things that can be seen, heard, felt, tasted, or known that would be useful.

An example is, 'And you may be becoming aware of a feeling as you relax,' or 'You could notice seeing things differently from now on.'

TIME

Using time presuppositionally is very powerful. If I say, 'As your confidence continues to grow', the word 'continues' shifts attention away from whether or not the client's confidence will grow, and presupposes that she has some level of confidence in the first place, which is a presupposition of existence. There are many words that can be used to adapt the client's perception of time: 'begin', 'end', 'stop', 'start', 'continue', 'proceed', 'already', 'yet', 'still', 'anymore'.

Can you see the difference between someone who says 'I haven't stopped smoking' and someone who says 'I haven't stopped smoking yet'? What does the second one presuppose? Have you seen how useful that could be to you as a therapist yet? What will have happened when you do? As you start to use time more than you are already, it will help you to continue in the improvement of your use of language.

ADVERB OR ADJECTIVE MODIFIERS

These shift attention away from the object of the sentence. For example, 'You could be surprised how easily you speak up at meetings.' The word 'easily' modifies the verb 'speak'. The effect is that attention moves onto the degree of ease they find in speaking, not on whether they will speak at the meeting at all.

Other examples might be 'in that comfortable chair' or 'just how quickly you change'. Modifiers are used all the time in advertising. Recently I drove past a Jaguar dealership that had a big sign saying 'Over 100 approved used vehicles'. Do you see how that subtly suggests that any Jaguar from anywhere else might be 'not approved'? In the next restaurant you visit read the menu. Will it say, 'Our steak has a bit of cheese on it, and some salad,' or 'Our succulent Aberdeen Angus steak has mature Stilton drizzled over it on a bed of mixed Mediterranean leaves.' Stop dribbling and keep reading.

Uses in therapy include, 'As you sit in the relaxing chair,' 'How quickly you're changing,' or 'How comfortably you're speaking to your boss.'

EXCLUSIVE OR

The presuppositional use of the word 'or' presents to the client the illusion of choice. A waitress once asked my son, 'Would you like peas or beans with your steak?' He replied, 'Peas, please.' As she walked away I said, 'But you don't like peas.' He said, 'I know, but I don't like beans either.' He didn't think of going to the third choice of neither, because the 'or' didn't suggest it. Most people's thinking remains within the box they are presented with most of the time. With a client you could say, 'I don't know whether you notice a big change in your behaviour or a small change,' or 'You may find it happening straightaway or a little later.' Once again we are not presenting a third choice of 'no change'. The client's attention shifts to the idea of the *degree* of change and so presupposes there will be some.

ORDINAL

Ordinal presuppositions are the use of the words 'first', 'second', 'third' etc., or the word 'next'. Saying to a client 'It may not be until the third time you speak comfortably that you realise how different you feel' presupposes there have been at least two other occasions when he spoke comfortably. Another example is: 'Whatever the next thing is you notice as you sink deeper' or 'And it may be the second time it happens that you notice it for the first time.' Notice how the latter presupposes there has been a first time and there will be a second time.

 EXISTENCE

The presupposition of existence may be best illustrated by a comparison. Read these three phrases:

Mike realised there was a tree behind the church.

Mike only just noticed there was a tree behind the church.

Mike didn't notice there was a tree behind the church.

Notice how the existence of several elements of those sentences are assumed, i.e. the existence of Mike, the church and the tree. Whether he does or doesn't notice the tree behind the church, the sentences all still presuppose the existence of the church, the tree and Mike. So if you say to a client, 'I don't know whether you'll notice how much better you are feeling as you talk to your audience,' it presupposes he's talking to the audience, and that he is feeling better.

➤ Presuppositional language can turn your suggestions into the most subtle and elegant of spells. It is fundamental to the effectiveness of Wordweaving.™ The exercise below gives you the chance to practise recognition of the presuppositional forms. Be aware that some may contain more than one presupposition. See how you get on. Answers on page 120. Think of some examples of your own.

1 You might be surprised at how easy you find relaxing.
2 Because you're relaxing you're learning.
3 You're sitting in this chair and that means you can relax.
4 Then you may find that you feel confident.
5 How soon things improve.
6 What you're aware of as you sink deeper.
7 And if you notice things changing then you'll know it's working.
8 And living is the same as learning.
9 You could notice things changing.
10 As you continue to improve.
11 How quickly you're changing.
12 How much easier you find things feeling.
13 I don't know whether your arms or legs feel heavier.
14 Those things you see in your mind as you let go.
15 Your mind can be open to new ideas because it's ready to be different.
16 Sitting in that comfortable chair.
17 What will have happened that you wanted to happen.
18 It doesn't matter whether you notice a big change, or a small one.
19 All the feelings you're noticing.
20 Whatever is the next thing you notice.
21 The thing that makes you realise you feel better.
22 When will be the first time it feels different.
23 The learning your unconscious takes from this session means you can notice many changes.
24 You might stop smoking today or tomorrow.

The Milton model

Let me begin with an apology. Most of the terms used in the Milton model are taken from transformational grammar and so appear mostly meaningless. Understanding what each aims to achieve is more important than remembering the label. The overriding principle is that the vagueness of the language causes the clients to search within their own model of the world for the meaning that is most pertinent to them, and does not depend on the therapist providing the meaning for them.

MIND READ

Claiming to know the thoughts or feelings of another without specifying the process by which you came to know the information.

'I wonder what you are feeling...' – this suggests you know they are feeling.

'I know that you are wondering....'

'We both know how important this is to you.'

LOST PERFORMATIVE

Value judgements, where the performer of the value judgement is left out. Lost performatives are an indicator of the beliefs that your client holds, usually

1 Possibility. 2 C>E. 3 Complex equivalence. 4 Possibility. 5 Time. 6 Awareness. 7 C>E. 8 Complex equivalence. 9 Possibility. 10 Time. 11 Time. 12 Modifier. 13 Exclusive or. 14 Awareness. 15 C>E. 16. Modifier. 17 Time. 18 Exclusive or. 19 Awareness. 20 Ordinal. 21 C>E. 22. Ordinal. 23 Complex equivalence. 24 Exclusive or.

unconsciously. As a therapist you can use them to introduce an idea as a positive thing, without giving evidence of why it is a good thing. It will be accepted as self-evident.

'It's right to relax deeply.'

'And it's a good thing to wonder.'

CAUSE AND EFFECT

Our good friend. Where it is implied that one thing causes another. Bandler and Grinder define three levels of causal connection or linkages:

The weakest kind of causal connection uses conjunctions like 'and' to link otherwise unrelated statements, such as,

'You can feel the comfortable chair and relax even more.'

The second level of causation uses words related to time , such as 'during', 'while', 'soon', 'as' and 'when', such as,

'As you allow your breathing to slow you sink even deeper.'

'Soon you may notice your eyelids becoming heavier while you listen to the music.'

The third level of linkage is the strongest and uses words like 'causes', 'requires', 'makes' or 'forces'.

'Each breath out makes you relax even deeper.'

The principle is to link something that is going on (like sitting, staring, blinking), with something you want them to achieve (like relaxing or feeling something different). Implied causatives include:

1   If... then.... 'If you notice how comfortable the chair is then you can relax even more.'

2   As you... then you.... 'As you feel more relaxed then you can know that you're growing more confident.'

COMPLEX EQUIVALENCE

Where two things are equated – as in their meanings being equivalent. 'That means....'

'You may notice colours on your eyelids, and that just means you're beginning to sink deeper.'

PRESUPPOSITION

The linguistic equivalent of assumptions, which we have already covered in depth.

'You are learning many things....'

UNIVERSAL QUANTIFIER

Excellent words that serve to generalise the client's experience, such as 'all', 'every', 'never', 'always', 'nobody', 'each', 'any'.

'And all the things, all the things....'

'And every, easy breath out helps you relax even more.'

'...feeling any feeling that lets you know...'

MODAL OPERATOR

Words that imply possibility or necessity, and that form our rules in life. Words like 'can', 'could', 'might', 'may', 'should', 'will'. Modal operators of possibility are very useful words for bypassing resistance, because they point out what it is possible to notice, not what the client is noticing or must notice:

'That you can learn.'

'That you might feel.'

'That you could notice.'

NOMINALISATIONS

These are process words that have been frozen in time by making them into nouns. Famously they are described as words acting as nouns that you couldn't put in a wheelbarrow, such as my 'relationship'. Use them with clients as signposts to guide them to a fuller understanding from their own deep structure, words such as 'knowledge', 'understanding', 'learning', 'resources', 'quality'.

'Provide you with new insights, and new understanding. '

'...what quality you could bring to this situation that would help to resolve it.'

UNSPECIFIED VERB

The use of words such as 'learn', 'know', 'understand', 'change', 'wonder', 'think', 'feel' gets the client to supply the meaning in order to understand the sentence.

'And you can... '

'And you might wonder how that feels...'

'And what you know...'

TAG QUESTION

A question added after a statement, which is designed to displace resistance.

'Can you not?'

'Haven't you?'

LACK OF REFERENTIAL INDEX

A corker of a ridiculous term. It simply means a phrase that does not specify the object the sentence alludes to, as in 'He broke it,' which does not specify who the 'he' is or what the 'it' is. This again causes the client to make sense of the sentence by providing the 'he' and 'it' from his or her own model of the world. The vagueness amplifies the possibilities of meaning.

'"This" is the way to understanding.'

'"It" could be really useful.'

COMPARATIVE DELETION (UNSPECIFIED COMPARISON)

Where a comparison is made and it is not specified what or whom the comparison is with.

'And it's more or less the right thing [according to whom?].'

'And you are so much more relaxed [than when?].'

'And it's so much better [than what?].'

PACE CURRENT EXPERIENCE

Where a client's experience (verifiable, external) is described in a way that is undeniable.

You are sitting here, listening to me, looking at me (etc.) [then linking it to your suggestion], as you relax more deeply while you are recognising....

BINDS

These come in two flavours, simple binds and double binds. A simple bind is the offer of a choice between two or more comparable alternatives, either of which takes the client in the direction you desire, often indistinguishable from the *exclusive or* (so don't bother trying):

'Would you relax more with your feet on the stool, or as you're sitting right now?'

'Will you find it easier to quit smoking straightaway or by the time you wake up tomorrow?'

As you can see, what is actually being offered is the illusion of choice, but the vast majority of clients will respond as if the choice is real. A variation of this is to offer all possibilities:

'As your arm relaxes you may find it getting heavier, or lighter, or it may even stay the same.'

'And tonight you may dream. They might be exciting dreams, strange dreams, funny dreams, normal dreams – or you may not even dream at all, and that will mean.... '

Double binds, on the other hand, offer possibilities of behaviour that are outside the client's conscious control. They suggest things that evoke an autonomic response at the unconscious level. There are several varieties, the following are a sample:

THE TIME DOUBLE BIND

These link an element of time to an autonomic response, like blushing, warmth, coolness, numbness, or ideomatic response.

'We can wonder just how soon that finger will move.'

'And at some point the pain will change to a new, easier sensation.'

An elegant example of a double bind used by Erickson was when he was working with a six-year-old boy:

'I know your father and mother have been asking you, Jimmy, to quit biting your nails. They don't seem to know that you're just a six-year-old boy. And they don't seem to know that you will naturally quit biting your nails just before you're seven years old. And they really don't know that! So when they tell you to stop biting your nails, just ignore them!'

THE CONSCIOUS-UNCONSCIOUS DOUBLE BIND

This has also been called the dissociation technique, and works by presupposing the existence of a conscious and unconscious mind. The key is to use words and context to split the function of the conscious and unconscious:

> 'You don't even need to listen to me because it is your unconscious that will be responding.'

> 'And we might wonder when you will notice the changes your unconscious is producing.'

> 'And whether you are aware of what your unconscious is learning or not doesn't actually matter.'

> 'And the understanding your unconscious has of what I am saying may be much more than you are aware of.'

THE DOUBLE-DISSOCIATION DOUBLE BIND

These involve a dissociation on two levels, which make conscious communication with your client possible during a trance induction:

> 'You can open your eyes and observe the pendulum as your unconscious causes it to move.'

> 'As you open your eyes and are able to communicate normally, your body remains fully and deeply relaxed.'

CONVERSATIONAL POSTULATE

The communication has the form of a question, a question to which the response is either a 'yes' or a 'no'. It allows the client to choose to respond or not and avoids authoritarianism.

'Do you feel this is something you understand?'

'Is this something you could imagine doing now?'

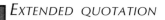

EXTENDED QUOTATION

Quotations are very useful because they separate the therapist from the information they are delivering. Quoting other clients is one example:

'I'm not surprised you feel this way because another client said to me [blah blah] and so....'

'A client said to me that she felt so much better once she had....'

By extending the quotation through several people the conscious mind tends to lose track (and interest), allowing the suggestion to be absorbed by the unconscious without critical interference. This is a useful technique I picked up from Gil Boyne, who said that when Milton Erickson had seen Bandler quote him as to how the unconscious really responds to extended quotations. Now then, without reading it again, who actually said that?

SELECTIONAL RESTRICTION VIOLATION

A sentence that is not well formed, in that animals or objects are given qualities they do not have, such as feelings.

'And the chair can feel you sinking deeper.'

'Your clothes can feel the warmth of your body as you....'

AMBIGUITY

Something is ambiguous if it can be understood in two or more possible senses. This again gives the client the freedom to make the sense of the ambiguity which is most useful to them in the context of their problem. A lot of comedy is based on ambiguity:

> A cowboy rides into a Wild West town and goes in to see the sheriff. He announces, 'I'm the meanest, roughest, toughest bounty hunter in the whole Wild West and I want you to give me the meanest, roughest, toughest outlaw to catch.' The sheriff leans back in his chair and says, 'Well, that'd be the Brown Paper Kid.' The stranger looks at him suspiciously, 'The Brown Paper Kid. Why'd they call him the Brown Paper Kid?' The sheriff replies, 'Well, he wears a brown paper hat, brown paper coat, brown paper chaps, brown paper boots. He's the Brown Paper Kid.' 'Okay, so what's he wanted for?' asks the bounty hunter. The sheriff pauses. 'Rustlin'!' [gratuitous inclusion of my favourite joke].

As with binds there are a number of distinctions:

A PHONOLOGICAL

Hear/here

> 'As your body is relaxing your mind can wander/ wonder where it would go that would be the safest and most relaxing place you've ever been.'

b Syntactic

Where the function (meaning) of a word cannot be immediately determined by the listener from the context it is used in.

'They are visiting relatives.'

'Flying planes can be dangerous.'

'Hypnotising hypnotists can be tricky.'

c Scope

Where it cannot be determined by the context how much of one part of the sentence applies to some other part.

'Speaking to you as a child.'

'The old men and women [are the women old as well?].'

'The disturbing noises and thoughts [are the thoughts disturbing?].'

'The weight of your hands and feet.'

d Punctuation

This is where two unrelated sentences or ideas are connected by a word that can sensibly fit into both parts, though usually the combination is ungrammatical (it won't matter).

'I want you to notice your [hand] me the glass.'

'You can take a [turn] that around in your life.'

UTILISATION

Utilise all that happens or is said.

A client says: 'I am not sure.' Response: 'That's right, you are not sure, yet, because you haven't asked the one question that will have you totally and completely sure.' The client shifts her body in the chair. 'That's right, and as your body makes itself even more comfortable you can...'.

EMBEDDED COMMANDS

By changing the cadence or intonation you can deliver a command in the middle of a sentence without it being identified as such by the conscious.

'And you might soon "stop smoking" because you find you want to.'

NEGATIVE SUGGESTIONS

Uses the idea of the blue-tree syndrome, by getting the client to think of something by telling him not to.

'I'm not saying that you'll notice a difference straightaway.'

Exercises

TASK: IDENTIFY THE LANGUAGE PATTERNS IN THE FOLLOWING —

'I know that you are thinking... and it's a good thing to think... because... that means... you are learning many things... and all the things, all the things... that you can learn... provide you with new insights, and new understandings. And you can, can you not? One can, you know. And it's more or less the right thing. You are sitting here, listening to me, looking at me, and that means that your unconscious mind is also here, and can hear what I say. And since that's the case, you are probably learning about this and already know more at an unconscious level than you think you do, and it's not right for me to tell him, learn this or learn that, let him learn in any way he wants, in any order. Do you feel this... is this something you understand? Because, last week I was with Gil who told me about his training in 1972 at Esalen when he talked to someone who said, "A chair can support you...".'

Using our direct examples from earlier, below are some possibilities of how the Milton model can be used to make the suggestion more elegant and convey its intention:

Mrs Toothbrush: 'When you see the toothbrush you notice all the things about it that make it useful and safe,' could become, 'When you see the toothbrush you could wonder how long you've thought of it now as something useful and safe.'

Mr Bachelor: 'As you converse with women you notice how relaxed they feel in your company and the way they look that lets you know they're enjoying the conversation,' could become, 'And it might not be until after you converse with women that you realise how much easier it felt to be relaxed as you enjoyed the conversation because of all the things that were different about you.'

Mrs Chocolate: 'In the supermarket you feel yourself finding the look of fruit more and more appealing,' could become, 'In the supermarket it doesn't matter whether apples or some other fruit are more appealing, and how much more you look forward to eating them when you remember it's time to eat only when you're hungry.'

Below are a number of examples of presuppositions and the Milton model. In the left column are the examples, on the right their category. Your task is twofold:

> 1 Cover the right column, read the examples in the left column, and identify the pattern. Practise this as many times as you like.

> 2 Underneath each example think of another.

1 I know that you are thinking...	Mind read
2 Many people think that this can be easy...	Lost performative
3 Because the chair is supporting you can feel many things...	C > E and a run-on sentence
4 And how much more you can learn...	Presupposition
5 The reason you feel relaxed is that you're ready to...	Complex equivalence
6 And everything you hear can help...	Universal quantifier
7 And you could learn...	Modal operator of possibility
8 To absorb this new learning...	Nominalisation
9 And you can feel the difference, can't you?	Tag question

10 And you can make many changes... — Unspecified verb

11 And that is one of those things... — Lack of referential index

12 And this is even easier to learn... — Comparative deletion

13 You're sitting in the chair, and hearing my voice as you close your eyes... — Pacing current experience

14 I don't know whether you'll see a small difference or a big difference... — Exclusive or

15 Can you close your eyes? — Conversational postulate

16 I heard this from Milton who told John that Virginia had thought that he was learning something new... — Extended quotations

17 This session is really looking exciting... — Selection restriction violation

18 It doesn't matter why you *stop smoking* from today... — Embedded command

19 Whether you feel as if you're floating or sinking or feel the same as you go into trance doesn't really matter... — All-range of possibilities

20 That's right, and as you
settle more comfortably in
the chair you can sink even
deeper...

Utilisation

21 The more you make the
muscles around your eyes
relax the more you notice
your eyelids heavier...

Single bind

22 I'm not saying that you'll
find this easy...

Negative suggestion

23 You can hear here but
from now on you will hear
there what is useful...

Phonological ambiguity

24 Fascinating people can be
difficult...

Syntactic ambiguity

25 And your heavy hands
and feet....

Scope ambiguity

26 I notice you are wearing a
watch carefully what I do...

Punctuation ambiguity

27 You realise you're sitting
in the chair...

Mind read

28 It's been proven that...

Lost performative

29 As you feel your arms
relaxing you can sink
deeper...

Cause and effect

30 Being in trance means...	Complex equivalence
31 Being even more relaxed...	Presupposition
32 All the things you notice... all the things...	Universal quantifiers
33 And you should realise...	Modal operator of necessity
34 And you can take this understanding with you...	Nominalisation
35 And things can be different, can't they?	Tag question
36 How you're relaxing...	Unspecified verb
37 And you can...	Lack of referential index
38 The best thing is...	Comparative deletion
39 We've talked, and you've told me many things while you've been sitting there.	Pacing current experience
40 It doesn't matter if you notice this now or later...	Double bind/exclusive or
41 Can you notice your hand in your lap...	Conversational postulate
42 As the chair feels you relaxing...	Selection restriction violation

43 As you continue to *relax more deeply* while you're listening...   Embedded command

44 And as you hear the car go by outside you can sink deeper as it fades...   Utilisation

45 The greater the feeling grows, the easier you find it to go into trance...   Single bind

46 Don't even think about how much better you'll feel...   Negative suggestion

47 Speaking to you as a child...   Syntactic ambiguity

48 And everything is still... changing.   Phonological ambiguity

49 The relaxing thoughts and noises...   Scope ambiguity

50 And as you look at the things you can see on your eyelids...   Mind read

51 It's been said that imagination is important...   Lost performative

52 And because you're here you can learn many things...   C > E

53 Change is natural...   Complex equivalence

54 Your growing abilities...	Presupposition, phonological (your, you are) ambiguity
55 And it's never the same case...	Universal quantifier
56 And you may find...	Modal operator of possibility
57 With the knowledge you carry with you...	Nominalisation
58 And things change, don't they...	Tag question
59 And now you know...	Unspecified verb
60 He told me what can help you now...	Lack of referential index
61 And it's even more true that...	Comparative deletion
62 The sound of the music , the feeling of the chair as you're listening to me...	Pacing experience
63 You could feel your left arm or right arm grow heavier...	Double bind
64 Can you imagine your eyelids heavier?	Conversational postulate
65 The pendulum can tell us what we need to know...	Selection restriction violation

66 If your mind were to have you *go there now*, where it would be that you could be enjoying letting go...?

Embedded command

67 The more often you hear my voice the easier you'll go into trance...

Single bind

68 Don't let yourself think of the memory connected to this event...

Negative suggestion

69 And you can let your mind wander around many things that help...

Phonological ambiguity (wonder/wander)

70 Changing people can be interesting...

Syntactic ambiguity

71 Your interesting thoughts and behaviour...

Scope ambiguity

Using states to guide suggestion

As a working definition *states* are what everyday people call feelings. I don't think we need to be any more complicated than that. From what you have read about emotions you already know the power that these things have over us, and the way the mind uses them for protection and evaluation. There are a number of ways of utilising states to change a client's perceptions, such as taking a client into the future and getting him to imagine how he feels having overcome his problem, or taking him back into the past to access a positive state (like confidence), which he can bring back to the present. The particular way I want to focus on using states involves the TP of post-hypnotic suggestion.

The principle behind post-hypnotic suggestion is that at some point in the future the clients' attention will be unconsciously drawn to something that can be therapeutically useful, like a difference in their behaviour or the behaviour of people around them, or a change in the feeling they get before giving a speech. Because the evidence for a difference or change in the future will be the evaluation that the client makes before, during, or after the event, it is sensible to make a positive state part of the post-hypnotic suggestion.

For example, instead of saying, 'You will feel more confident as you walk into the room' [direct], or 'You may notice whatever the difference is as you walk into the room that makes you realise you feel more confident' [indirect], you could use one of a number of useful states, such as,

'You might be *surprised* to notice the difference as you walk into the room that makes you realise you feel more confident.'

'You might be *amazed* to notice the difference as you walk into the room that makes you realise you feel more confident.'

'The difference as you walk into the room that makes you realise you feel more confident could make you *smile* as you notice it.'

There are many states that can be utilised in this way, ones that I have found to be particularly useful are:

surprise	amazement	curiosity
amusement	anticipation	wondering

This list is far from comprehensive, as there are many others that can be used. The principle behind it is that we know how we are by how we feel. So if we can use a combination of sensory distortion and post-hypnotic suggestion to create a feeling that dominates the client's awareness at the moment a problem would normally arise, then it blocks what would normally be the dominant negative feeling/emotion. By changing the emotion within the Matrix Model of the problem it changes the problem itself. In essence you are suggesting a feeling to occur at a particular moment that absorbs enough attention to nullify any negative feeling that would normally be present.

An example is one I used with the woman whose obsessive compulsion ensured she checked she had turned her lamps out sixteen times:

'And you may be *surprised* the first time you walk away from a lamp knowing that you have checked it only twice....'

'And you could find it hard not to *smile* at the thought that you've done it so easily every time you're doing it from today.'

If we go back to our three long-suffering clients:

Mrs Toothbrush already uses a feeling to guide her perception: 'When you see the toothbrush you could *wonder* how long you've thought of it now as something useful and safe.'

Mr Bachelor: 'And it might not be until after you converse with women that you realise how much easier it felt to be relaxed as you enjoyed the conversation because of all the things that were different about you' could become 'And you might be *surprised* that it's not until after your conversation with the women that you realise how much easier it felt to be relaxed and you could be *curious* about the differences that made it so much more enjoyable.'

Notice how the use of these states enables the first part of the suggestion to be made in a direct form without it appearing direct.

Mrs Chocolate: 'In the supermarket it doesn't matter whether apples or some other fruits are more appealing, and how much more you look forward to eating them when you remember it's time to eat only when you're hungry' could become, 'We can both *wonder* whether apples or some other fruit appear more appealing in the supermarket, and you could be *amused* at how much more you look forward to eating them when you remember it's time to eat only when you're hungry.'

TASK

Look back at some of the suggestions you have created so far and adjust them to include one or more post-hypnotic state. Remember to use them with the presupposition of possibility – 'you could be amazed,' not 'you will be...'.

The Three Steps of Wordweaving™

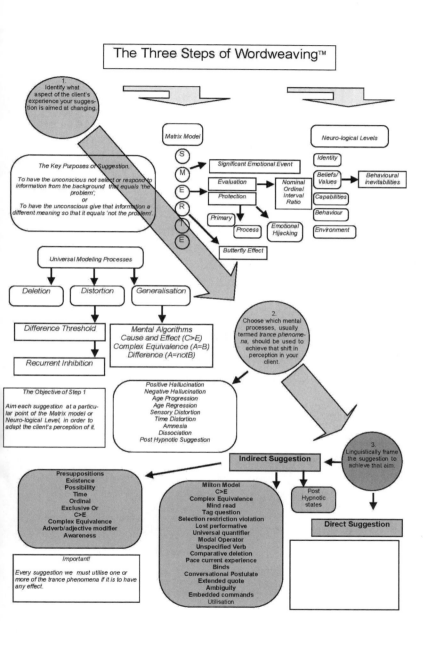

1. Identify what aspect of the client's experience your suggestion is aimed at changing.

Matrix Model

Neuro-logical Levels

The Key Purposes of Suggestion.

To have the unconscious not select or respond to information from the background that equals 'the problem';
or
To have the unconscious give that information a different meaning so that it equals 'not the problem'.

S
M
E
R
T
E

Significant Emotional Event

Evaluation
Protection

Nominal
Ordinal
Interval
Ratio

Primary

Process

Emotional
Hijacking

Butterfly Effect

Identity
Beliefs/
Values
Capabilities
Behaviour
Environment

Behavioural
inevitabilities

Universal Modeling Processes

Deletion | Distortion | Generalisation

Difference Threshold

Recurrent Inhibition

*Mental Algorithms
Cause and Effect (C>E)
Complex Equivalence (A=B)
Difference (A=notB)*

2. Choose which mental processes, usually termed *trance phenomena*, should be used to achieve that shift in perception in your client.

The Objective of Step 1

Aim each suggestion at a particular point of the Matrix model or Neuro-logical Level, in order to adapt the client's perception of it.

*Positive Hallucination
Negative Hallucination
Age Progression
Age Regression
Sensory Distortion
Time Distortion
Amnesia
Dissociation
Post Hypnotic Suggestion*

3. Linguistically frame the suggestion to achieve that aim.

Indirect Suggestion

Presuppositions
Existence
Possibility
Time
Ordinal
Exclusive Or
C>E
Complex Equivalence
Adverb/adjective modifier
Awareness

Milton Model
C>E
Complex Equivalence
Mind read
Tag question
Selection restriction violation
Lost performative
Universal quantifier
Modal Operator
Unspecified Verb
Comparative deletion
Pace current experience
Binds
Conversational Postulate
Extended quote
Ambiguity
Embedded commands
Utilisation

Post
Hypnotic
states

Direct Suggestion

Important!

Every suggestion we must utilise one or more of the trance phenomena if it is to have any effect.

Part IV

Putting it all together

Now you have had the opportunity to practise the three separate components of Wordweaving™ it is time to put them together. You have learnt that our mind gives meaning to what is happening to us, and around us, by making three kinds of comparisons with past information:

1. Cause and effect comparison – as in 'I feel this way about what is happening because of what happened to me in the past.'

2. Complex equivalence comparison – where 'this current thing is the same, or has the same meaning as a past thing.'

or

3. A difference comparison – when 'the current information is perceived as being different from past information.'

This gives us the point of our suggestions – to use TP and language patterns to guide the clients' attention in such a way as to build a new comparison between their future experiences and their problem experiences in the past. The point of the new comparison is to notice a difference or change in how they perceive these future events as they occur, and use that difference or change to build a new belief about themselves and/or the world.

This means that within a session, which might contain dozens of different suggestions, the ratio of where you aim the suggestions within the clients' Neuro-logical Levels should be something like this:

 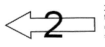

20-30% of your suggestions should link these changes to a new meaning the client can build *(a new belief)* about the themselves *(identity)* and the world they live in.

Fig 7

70-80% of your suggestions should be aimed at the client achieving a change in their perception of their environment *(the stimulus and their emotional feeling to it)*, or their behaviour *(their response)*, or the resources they have to respond to it with *(capabilities)*

IMPORTANT!

Twenty to thirty per cent of your suggestions should be aimed at linking the suggestions you make regarding their environment, their capabilities, or their behaviour, to a change in the beliefs or sense of identity of your clients.

As I began to explain in Part I, the link between one and two (in the diagram above) is formed by the use of new C>E and complex equivalence suggestions. For example the following pattern is aimed at environment, behaviour and capabilities:

'...and so you may begin to notice the difference before you walk into the meeting... or as you enter the room... that could leave you surprised at how much better you respond to the other people... in a way that makes you aware of the ease that you feel when you know what you are talking about.'

If now I want to link those suggestions to the client's belief system or identity to give a meaning to the client to transform her perception of such events, I might add:

'And that means that in the future you could increasingly recognise what a good speaker you are [identity], and know [belief] that people are ready to listen to the useful things you have to say.'

That is using a complex equivalence language form, i.e. previous suggestions *mean* the outcome of the next suggestion. Alternatively I could phrase it as a C > E:

'And because of those changes you might not even be aware of when you first realise what a good speaker you are, and as you do, how much more you begin to look forward to those opportunities to communicate as clearly as you know you can.'

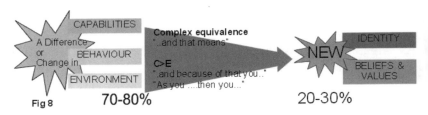

Fig 8

70-80%   20-30%

Overall, the above demonstrates what your session should be aiming to achieve. I stipulate the ratio of seventy to thirty per cent, not intending that you strictly measure your suggestions, only to remind you that if you repeatedly suggest a change in the client's beliefs or identity, without evidence to validate those suggestions, they will seldom have an effect. Linking roughly four suggestions of change or difference in environment, behaviour and capability (the evidence) to one new meaning about the client's identity or beliefs, tends to give an effective balance and avoids resistance in the client.
In this way Wordweaving™ uses all three of the algorithms the mind uses to create meaning in a specific sequence to create a new meaning. We are using the mechanism that creates the problem to dissolve the problem – spell versus counter-spell. Now all we are left to do is master the skill of how to generate the suggestions that form the counter-spell. That is largely a matter of practice, so let's make a start. Wordweaving™ involves listening to the client in order to establish:

1   Is there a particular Neuro-logical Level or point of the Matrix Model that acts as a focus for the client's problem?

2   What TP create the problem?

In the following case studies, for the sake of brevity, I have paraphrased into a short paragraph the information a client might give you over the course of an interview.

CASE STUDY ONE

> Client: 'I don't know really, I start off being good, but then if I know there's chocolate in the house I just can't stop thinking about it, and if I'm stressed or upset I want to eat, it's comforting, isn't it? Afterwards it makes me feel bad because I see myself getting fatter. I just have no willpower.'

Let's examine the information available from what she's told us:

> '...if I know there's chocolate in the house I just can't stop thinking about it...'

So, as usual, the environment supplies the stimulus – the chocolate, and she positively hallucinates the bar of chocolate wherever in the house she is.

> '...if I'm stressed or upset I want to eat, it's comforting, isn't it?'

At the Neuro-logical Level of belief the client holds the complex equivalence of food equals comfort (generalisation of meaning relationship, page 33). The sentence also provides you with a stimulus for when she needs comfort – whenever she has the feelings (Matrix Model – emotion) of stress or upset.

> 'Afterwards it makes me feel bad because I see myself getting fatter.'

Age progression occurs after eating because she sees herself as fatter in the future (possibly with a number of added consequences, such as loneliness), which is likely to provide the stress stimulus that will return her to her source of comfort – and so the cycle continues.

'I just have no willpower.'

Another belief (of helplessness, see page 35), and also a post-hypnotic suggestion that ensures that the conditions exist for the cycle to continue.

We have now established that her stimuli for eating are: being aware of chocolate around her, and the emotions of stress and upset. The TP she uses include positive hallucination, age progression, and post-hypnotic suggestion. I say 'include' because they are identifiable. Others might be implied, such as the negative hallucination of everything else but the chocolate, the sensory distortion of getting a bad feeling from eating what she likes, and the amnesia for those times in her life when she has had willpower.

THE THREE STEPS OF WORDWEAVING™

1 Identify what aspect of the client's experience your suggestion is aimed at changing.

2 Choose which mental process, among those usually termed 'trance phenomena', should be used to achieve the shift in perception in your client.

3 Linguistically frame the suggestion to achieve that aim.

With the information from the client, we have what we need to follow the first two steps of Wordweaving.™ We can then begin to aim our suggestions at the parts of the problem, making sure we use the TP that cause the problem, as well as any others that come to mind and seem appropriate.

With step three we now frame the suggestion to achieve the aim. If stated directly the suggestion could be (only 'could' because there is a wide range of possibility. Please never think that the suggestions I propose are the only ones that would work):

1 Direct suggestion: 'From today you forget about chocolate, you think only about healthy, slimming foods. Whenever you think about needing food you see these healthy, slimming foods. You recognise that eating too much stresses you more so you find that eating less is comforting because you can see yourself in the future slimmer, and feeling good about yourself.'

This suggestion pattern includes:

'...you forget about chocolate' – amnesia

Whenever you think about needing food you see these healthy, slimming foods – positive hallucination

'...eating too much stresses you more...' – introduces a new belief

'...eating less is comforting...' – introduces a new complex equivalence (less equals comfort)

'...because you can see yourself in the future slimmer, and feeling good about yourself...' – the word 'because' turns the complex equivalence into the cause part of a C>E statement, where the effect of *less* equals *comfort* is an age progression to her feeling slimmer and better about herself

If you compare the information from the client you can see that each one of her three points is addressed within the above suggestion pattern, and that there are roughly four suggestions operating at the levels of environment, behaviour and capability, and one suggestion about identity/belief linked by a C > E and complex equivalence.

2 Indirect suggestion: If we take the ideas from 1. (above) and use presuppositions and Milton model patterns we can layer in more subtle levels of suggestion:

> 'From today you may be surprised at how easy it is to forget chocolate for longer and longer periods. It might not be until the end of the day that you look back and realise how you've been noticing healthy food so much more. And we can wonder when will be the first time that you notice how comforting it is to know that what you're eating is helping you to lose weight, and knowing that you can means that you're learning something new about what you can achieve, and you might not totally believe yet that you have all the willpower you need to succeed, until that moment when you know it's true... now... it's true that that means there is so much to look forward to in the future... so many things because you're slimmer... feeling so much better about yourself... so many opportunities and possibilities....'

You might notice the possibilities that exist by using indirect suggestion. Let's look at the language patterns and TP used, and where the suggestions were aimed:

'from today' – presupposition of time

'you may' – presupposition of possibility

'be surprised at' – post-hypnotic suggestion

'how easy it is to forget chocolate' – adverb modifier (of forget); TP equals amnesia

'for longer and longer periods' – TP equals time distortion

'it might' – presupposition of possibility

'not be until the end of the day that you look back' – negative suggestion TP equals time distortion

'and realise' – presupposition of awareness

'how you've been noticing healthy food so much more' – presupposition of awareness; logical levels of environment and behaviour; adjective modifier

'and we can wonder when will be the first time that' – presupposition of possibility; ordinal presupposition

'you notice how comforting' – presupposition of awareness; adverb modifier; logical level of behaviour (noticing)

'it is to know that what you're eating is helping you to lose weight' – C > E (what you're eating to lose weight is causing the feeling of comfort), TP equals sensory distortion; working on the logical level of belief

'and knowing that you can means that you're learning something new about what you can achieve' – presupposition of possibility; complex equivalence; unspecified verb (learning); presupposition of possibility; logical level of belief (you can)

'and you might not totally believe yet that you have all the willpower you need to succeed, until that moment when you know it's true...' – negative suggestion; presupposition of time (yet); universal quantifier (all) presupposition of time; logical level of belief...

'now... it's true that that means there is so much to' – presupposition of time; lost performative (it's true); complex equivalence

'look forward to in the future... so many things because you're slimmer... feeling so much better about yourself... so many opportunities and possibilities...' – TP equals age progression; lack of referential index (things); TP equals post-hypnotic suggestion (slimmer, feeling better); logical level of identity (yourself)

This examination is not exhaustive, as I am sure you will find some I have missed – which is good, it shows you're listening, and that means.... Notice again the one-to-four ratio in terms of Neuro-logical Levels.

CASE STUDY TWO

> Client: 'I have no confidence. I'm not assertive, so people walk all over me and make me feel small. Meeting new people makes me panic and I can see they think I'm weird. Unless I get over this I can't ever see myself meeting a partner.'

What information is the client giving us?

'I have no confidence.'

A common introduction. The client is representing the problem at the level of belief, maybe even identity (if, for example, he had said, 'I am someone with no confidence.').

'I'm not assertive, so people walk all over me and make me feel small.'

Now the client moves to the level of capability – he doesn't 'do' assertiveness. People acting in a way that causes him to feel they are dominating him triggers an age regression to the point where he feels small. A cause-and-effect situation – dominant behaviour (his perception) causes him to regress. Within the Matrix Model this helps us to identify one stimulus as being this kind of perceived behaviour that leads to the emotion connected to feeling small.

'Meeting new people makes me panic and I can see they think I'm weird.'

Another C > E. New people 'make him' panic – another stimulus that elicits an emotional response. He produces a positive hallucination whereby he sees them seeing him as he sees himself – weird. The structure of this problem is probably that of the stimulus of new people causing him to age progress ('Oh no, they're going to think I'm weird!'), which causes the flight response, which he interprets as a panic attack, which generates the evaluation of him acting weird in the company of new people. The therapeutic paradox again, his behaviour creating the impression he is trying to avoid.

> 'Unless I get over this I can't ever see myself meeting a partner.'

The client has a complex equivalence whereby having no confidence means he cannot establish a relationship – a useful post-hypnotic suggestion that will neatly sabotage any new liaison. The continuation of this belief generates an age progression where he sees himself alone. As usual, the presence of a complex equivalence indicates the client operating at the Neuro-logical Level of belief.

With this client we have the TP of age progression, age regression and positive hallucination. The stimuli that generate the context of his 'no confidence' are people dominating him, or meeting new people. In the Matrix Model the unconscious evaluation is that his lack of confidence makes people think he's weird and will keep him single.

What suggestions could we make?

1 Direct suggestion: 'As you approach new people you remain relaxed and calm, you talk normally and easily. Whenever people attempt to walk all over you you notice yourself only remaining tall, acting your age, and speaking firmly about your needs. With this new confidence you will find that you approach people feeling more attractive, remaining calm and knowing you appear perfectly normal to them.'

This suggestion pattern includes:

'As you approach new people you remain relaxed and calm, you talk normally and easily' – post hypnotic suggestion

'Whenever people attempt to walk all over you you notice yourself only remaining tall, acting your age, and speaking firmly about your needs' – negative hallucination (noticing only the positive will mean he doesn't notice any other feelings he might have)

'With this new confidence you will find that you approach people feeling more attractive' – sensory distortion

'...remaining calm and knowing you appear perfectly normal to them' – positive hallucination (the client will hallucinate how he looks normal to the other person, a form of dissociation)

2 Indirect suggestion: 'And it's always possible to learn something new... about confidence... about people... meeting each other you may find yourself noticing how nervous they might be feeling at first, and curious about why they might be feeling you need to put them at ease... doing whatever you find yourself doing to accomplish that... and as you make it easier for them you could find your confidence growing from knowing how you're helping them... so focused you don't even notice how you're feeling better until later... and it doesn't matter how much you stand up for yourself the first time... only that as you notice you have you can easily believe that it's possible to do it even more the next time... so as time passes and your ability grows with your confidence you might hear yourself really believing, "I am a more and more confident person."'

Go through the suggestion pattern and see if you can work out the levels, TP and language, and then compare it with below:

'And it's always possible to learn something new '– universal quantifier; lack of referential index; aimed at Neuro-logical Level of capability

'...about confidence... about people...' – beginning to link what they learn about people to gaining confidence

'meeting each other you may find yourself noticing '– presuppositions of possibility and awareness; Neuro-logical Level of environment

'how nervous they might be feeling at first' – positive hallucination; presupposition of possibility

'and curious about why they might be feeling *you need to put them at ease...*' – mind read; embedded command; Neuro-logical Level of behaviour

'doing whatever you find yourself doing to accomplish that...' – unspecified verb; Neuro-logical Level of behaviour

'and as you make it easier for them you could find your confidence growing from knowing how you're helping them...' – presupposition of possibility; complex equivalence; Neuro-logical Level of capability

'so focused you don't even notice how you're feeling better until later... '– TP equals negative hallucination linked to time distortion

'and it doesn't matter how much you stand up for

yourself the first time...' – TP equals negative suggestion; ordinal; presupposition of existence (of standing up); Neuro-logical Level of capability

'only that as you notice you have' – presuppositions of awareness and time

'you can easily believe that it's possible to do it even more the next time...' – adverb modifier; presupposition of possibility and time; Neuro-logical Level of belief

'so as time passes' – presupposition of time

'and your ability grows with your confidence' – complex equivalence; Neuro-logical Level of capability

'you might hear yourself really believing "I am a more and more confident person"' – presupposition of possibility; TP equals sensory distortion; C > E aimed at Neuro-logical Levels of belief and identity

In the next case I'll give you more to do.

CASE STUDY THREE

Client: 'Ever since my children left home I've felt really depressed. I just can't see the point to anything. I used really to enjoy gardening and dancing, but I just can't be bothered. I can see my friends are getting fed up with me, which makes me withdraw even more, I'm just no use to anybody.'

Look at the above and identify the information the client is giving us, as I did in the first two examples. Write it in the box provided and then compare it with what is below (no peeking).

'Ever since my children left home I've felt really depressed '– cause and effect. TP equals possible time distortion and amnesia/negative hallucination (has she constantly been depressed, every day?)

'I just can't see the point to anything '– negative hallucination; universal quantifier about behaviour

'I used really to enjoy gardening and dancing, but I just can't be bothered' – Neuro-logical Level of behaviour; TP equals age regression

'I can see my friends are getting fed up with me' – TP equals possible positive hallucination; mind read

'...which makes me withdraw even more' – C > E; TP equals dissociation

'I'm just no use to anybody' – Neuro-logical Level of belief/identity

Now write out four direct suggestions aimed at environment, behaviour, or capability. Then write out a complex equivalence or C > E aimed at belief or identity.

Now translate the above into indirect form using the Milton model and presuppositions, maintaining their aim, and identifying the TP involved.

My direct suggestions might be:

You begin to notice the beauty in the garden and do something each day to improve it.

And remembering how much you used to enjoy the company of your friends you realise how much they need you.

And because it's lonely to dance alone you find how useful you are to your partner.

From today you find new points to your days, moving on.

And because you're moving on it means that you feel you are a useful person, and you do believe there is a point to the things you do as you notice the pleasure you give to people.

Indirectly this might translate to:

'And it can be easy sometimes to notice suddenly the simple beauty in the garden, and the things to do to maintain it that make you realise how important your expertise is to that beauty, and we can both wonder what other things come to your mind as you enjoy doing those small important jobs in the garden that can give your day a point... as you may even realise how much your friendship means to those who need it... and how much you have enjoyed that interaction... as you daydream about those good times again in the future... looking back on a productive day and realising how it's flown... that there may even be a time soon when you have to organise your days around your dancing, because it's important to your partners that they are not detached from the fun you're having....'

'And because of those important things you want to bother to do you might be surprised when you first realise how much better you're feeling as you look forward to bothering because you know you're important to many people... which means you're useful... doesn't it?'

Now the trainer wheels come off and you can fly solo (mixed metaphor, I know). On the following pages are some more opportunities to build your confidence and expertise at Wordweaving.™ With such practice you will be surprised how quickly you find yourself listening for the information you need and unconsciously formulating it into the Wordweaving™ system, and you may be surprised to begin with at the things you hear yourself say that you recognise as excellent counter-spells.

 CASE STUDY FOUR

Client: 'I smoke most when I'm stressed because it calms me down. I can go for hours if I'm relaxed, or if I know I can't smoke – such as on a plane – I just forget about them, but if I get anxious I reach for the packet. I want to give up now though because I caught my little girl pretending to smoke and I can see her becoming a smoker if I don't quit.'

Look at the above and identify the information the client is giving us:

'I smoke most when I'm stressed because it calms me down' – C>E; Neuro-logical Level of belief; sensory distortion (cigarettes don't calm)

'I can go for hours if I'm relaxed, or if I know I can't smoke' – such as on a plane – logical level of belief; possible TP equals time distortion

'I just forget about them' – TP equals amnesia

'...but if I get anxious I reach for the packet' – stimulus is stress/anxiety; complex equivalence (anxiety means I need to smoke)

'I want to give up now though because I caught my little girl pretending to smoke and I can see her becoming a smoker if I don't quit' – TP equals age progression; motivation for change

Now write out four direct suggestions aimed at environment, behaviour, or capability. Then write out a complex equivalence or C>E aimed at belief or identity.

Now translate the above into indirect form using the Milton model and presuppositions, maintaining their aim, and identifying the TP involved.

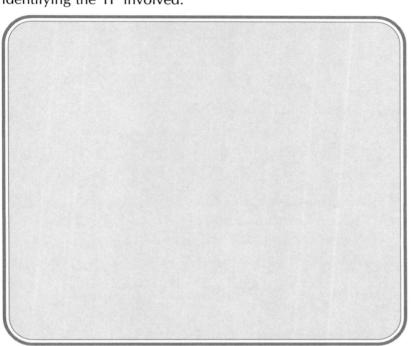

 CASE STUDY FIVE

Client: 'I'm terrified of flying. Every time I hear a change in the engine, or we hit turbulence, I think "That's it, we're going to crash," and I see us plummeting to the ground. I know how safe planes are really, but I forget all that whenever we're off the ground and something happens.'

Look at the above and identify the information the client is giving us:

'I'm terrified of flying' – Neuro-logical Level of belief; emotion of terror

'Every time I hear a change in the engine, or we hit turbulence I think "That's it, we're going to crash," and I see us plummeting to the ground' – the generalisation of 'every' suggests amnesia or negative hallucination of those sounds or times when she hasn't responded in this way; C>E, engine noise or turbulence triggers the effect of the belief it means the plane will crash; age progression and positive hallucination

'I know how safe planes are really, but I forget all that whenever we're off the ground and something happens' – amnesia of the resources she has

Now write out four direct suggestions aimed at environment, behaviour, or capability. Then write out a complex equivalence or C>E aimed at belief or identity.

Now translate the above into indirect form using the Milton model and presuppositions, maintaining their aim, and identifying the TP involved.

Conclusion

There is nothing new under the sun, and the various models that Wordweaving™ has sought to integrate have been available for many years, but then so were the ingredients of gunpowder before someone thought to mix them. I had a number of reasons for writing this book. One was that I just love this subject. The pursuit of its secrets has been my passion for the last ten years. I hope that this book might begin to fuel the same passion in you, because the subject needs people with passion and intense curiosity like never before.

At this time hypnotherapy has the possibility of moving to another level, not just in terms of acceptance by the medical community and the public, but also in terms of what it could offer in the field of mind/body medicine. Evidence is already available as to the power of hypnosis, but I do not think it will fulfil its potential if we do not rigorously pursue this field as a science. I do not believe that doing so will rob the subject of its mysticism, but will make it more accessible to a wider range of people, and help us make its use more effective. Its expert use may appear an art, but if it has an effect on the recipient then there is a psychological principle behind it, and understanding such principles must make us more accurate in our use of trance. I hope that the principles in Wordweaving™ will help in the development of this accuracy, and hopefully lead to something even better. Now is the time to move hypnotherapy towards a recognition of its legitimate place, particularly now that science is providing us with evidence of the scale of its effect.

Dr Spiegel at Stanford University hooked up hypnotised students to a brain-imaging machine and had them look at a black and white object while being told it was coloured. The parts of the brain that became active were the parts that process colour. In the students' reality the object was coloured.[29]

Think about that, because it is the reason I devoted so much space to explaining the way we create our version of the world. Hypnosis changed the students' perception of their reality. In their world black and white *were* colour, not just an illusion. Hypnosis can change our reality.

As such it holds the possibility of helping people create their best possible reality. Who knows what it could achieve? Could changing a client's perception of an illness affect its reality? There are many who already believe that their thoughts affect their health, that the body eavesdrops and responds to negativity with illness and disease. Some claim a direct causal link. Time will tell, and I hope hypnotherapy plays an integral part in the telling.

I hope Wordweaving™ provides you with a means of improving your ability to help people. Even more, I hope it ignites the passion in you that has made writing this such a pleasure for me.

The Three Steps of Wordweaving™

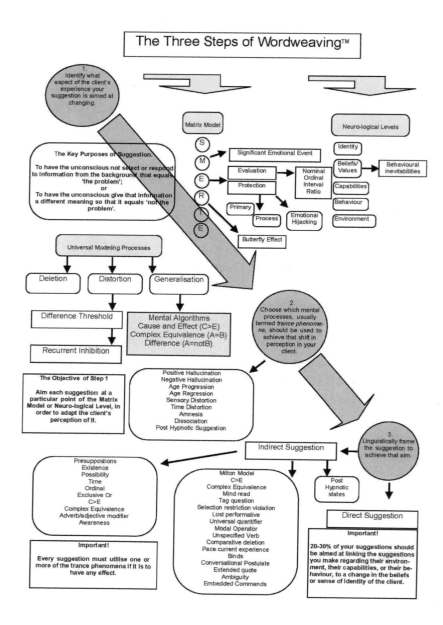

1. Identify what aspect of the client's experience your suggestion is aimed at changing.

Matrix Model

- S
- M
- E
- R
- T
- E

The Key Purposes of Suggestion.

To have the unconscious not select or respond to information from the background that equals 'the problem';
or
To have the unconscious give that information a different meaning so that it equals 'not the problem'.

Significant Emotional Event

Evaluation → Nominal Ordinal Interval Ratio

Protection

Primary

Process → Emotional Hijacking

Butterfly Effect

Neuro-logical Levels

- Identity
- Beliefs/Values → Behavioural inevitabilities
- Capabilities
- Behaviour
- Environment

Universal Modeling Processes

- Deletion
- Distortion
- Generalisation

Difference Threshold

Recurrent Inhibition

Mental Algorithms
Cause and Effect (C>E)
Complex Equivalence (A=B)
Difference (A=notB)

2. Choose which mental processes, usually termed *trance phenomena*, should be used to achieve that shift in perception in your client.

The Objective of Step 1

Aim each suggestion at a particular point of the Matrix Model or Neuro-logical Level, in order to adapt the client's perception of it.

Positive Hallucination
Negative Hallucination
Age Progression
Age Regression
Sensory Distortion
Time Distortion
Amnesia
Dissociation
Post Hypnotic Suggestion

3. Linguistically frame the suggestion to achieve that aim.

Indirect Suggestion

Presuppostions
Existence
Possibility
Time
Ordinal
Exclusive Or
C>E
Complex Equivalence
Adverb/adjective modifier
Awareness

Milton Model
C>E
Complex Equivalence
Mind read
Tag question
Selection restriction violation
Lost performative
Universal quantifier
Modal Operator
Unspecified Verb
Comparative deletion
Pace current experience
Binds
Conversational Postulate
Extended quote
Ambiguity
Embedded Commands

Post Hypnotic states

Direct Suggestion

Important!

Every suggestion must utilise one or more of the trance phenomena if it is to have any effect.

Important!

20-30% of your suggestions should be aimed at linking the suggestions you make regarding their environment, their capabilities, or their behaviour, to a change in the beliefs or sense of identity of the client.

Notes

1 Miller, GA, 'The Magical Number Seven, Plus or minus Two', in *Psychological Review*, no 63 (1956), pp81–87.
2 Wolinsky, S, *Trances People Live*, The Bramble Company (1991), pp62–63.
3 Norretranders, T, *The User Illusion*, Penguin Books (1998), pp178–210.
4 Korzybski, A, *Science and Sanity*, Institute of General Semantics (1995), pp58–60.
5 Bandler, R and Grinder, J, *The Structure of Magic*, vol 1, Science and Behavior Books (1975), p179.
6 Huxley, A, *The Doors of Perception*, Flamingo (1996) pp22–23.
7 Atkinson, R, Smith and Benn, *Introduction to Psychology*,11th edn, Harcourt Brace College Publishers (1991), p129.
8 Ibid, pA-51.
9 James, T, *Prime Concerns* (1996), pp7–15.
10 Penfield, W, *The Mystery of the Mind: A Critical Study of Consciousness and the Human Brain*, Princeton University Press (1975).
11 Wilson, RA, *Prometheus Rising*, New Falcon Publications (1999), p25.

12   Dilts, R, *Changing Belief Systems With NLP*, Meta publications Ltd (1990).
13   Bateson, G, *Steps to an Ecology of Mind*, University of Chicago Press (1972).
14   Wolinsky, op cit, pp16–17.
15   Dilts, op cit, p25.
16   Carter, R, *Mapping the Mind*, Weidenfield and Nicholson (1998), pp81–83.
17   Piaget, J, *The Child's Conception of the World*, Rowman and Littlefield (1990).
18   LeDoux, J, *The Emotional Brain*, Phoenix (1998).
19   Goleman, G, *Emotional Intelligence*, Bloomsbury Publishers plc (1996).
20   Evans, D, and Zarate, O, *Introducing Evolutionary Psychology*, Icon Books (1999).
21   Boyne, G, *Transforming Therapy*, Westwood Publishers (1989), p376.
22   Norretranders, op cit, p6.
23   Gleick, J, *Chaos. Making a New Science*, Penguin Books (1988), pp11–31.
24   Wolinsky, op cit.
25   Talbot, Michael, *The Holographic Universe*, Harper Collins (1991), pp74–76.
26   Brown, JAC, *Freud and the Post-Freudians*, Penguin Books (1991).
27   Bandler and Grinder, op cit.
28   James, T, *NLP Practitioner Manual* (1997).
29   Spiegel, D, from a speech given to the American Association for the Advancement of Science, reported in *The Guardian*, 18th February 2002.

Bibliography

Bateson, G, *Steps to an Ecology of Mind*.
Rubin, B and South, T, *Ericksonian Approaches*.
John, B and Bodenhammer, B, *Hypnotic Language*.
Candace, P, *The Molecules of Emotion*.

Index

Wordweaving™

The Science of Suggestion

To assist people in honing their use of hypnotic language we provide a range of further learning aids, including a card game, and an audio CD. To discover more please access our website:

www.wordweaving.co.uk

or contact our office:

The Quest Institute
Berkley House
Bower Way
Cippenham
Slough
Berks SL1 5HW

Tel: 01753 693630

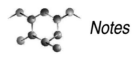 *Notes*

PRACTICE -

Notes   _Exercises_ - P. 67/61

P. 118

p. 68/69   see 31.   A=70.

 *Notes*

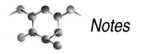 *Notes*

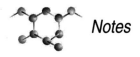 *Notes*

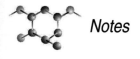 *Notes*

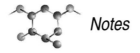 *Notes*